LION BRAND®

JUSTSOCKS

Also by Lion Brand Yarn
Lion Brand Yarn: Just Wraps
Lion Brand Yarn: Just Bags
Lion Brand Yarn: Just Gifts
Lion Brand Yarn: Just Hats
Lion Brand Yarn: Just Scarves
Lion Brand Yarn: Vintage Styles for Today

LION BRAND® YARN

JUST SOCKS

FAVORITE PATTERNS TO KNIT AND CROCHET

EDITED BY SHANNON OKEY

POTTER
CRAFT

NEW YORK

The authors and publisher would like to thank the Craft Yarn
Council of America for providing the yarn weight standards
and accompanying icons used in this book. For more
information, please visit www.YarnStandards.com.

Published in the United States by Potter Craft,
an imprint of the Crown Publishing Group,
a division of Random House, Inc., New York
www.crownpublishing.com
www.pottercraft.com

POTTER CRAFT and CLARKSON N. POTTER are trademarks,
and POTTER and colophon are registered trademarks of
Random House, Inc.

Library of Congress Cataloging-in-Publication Data
Just socks : favorite patterns to knit and crochet /
edited by Shannon Okey. — 1st ed.
      p. cm.
  At head of title: Lion Brand Yarn
  Includes index.
  ISBN 978-0-307-34595-0
  1. Knitting—Patterns. 2. Socks. I. Okey, Shannon,
1975- II. Lion Brand Yarn (Company) III. Title: Lion
Brand Yarn. IV. Title: Lion Brand Yarn just socks.

  TT825.J868 2007
  746.43'2041—dc22
                                    2007010005
Printed in Mexico

Design by Rebecca Pollock
Photography by Jack Deutsch

Library of Congress Cataloging-in-Publication

ISBN: 978-0-307-34595-0

10 9 8 7 6 5 4 3 2 1

First Edition

CONTENTS

INTRODUCTION

From the ordinary crew sock to complex cables and lace, socks are a part of almost everyone's daily outfit. Stuck in a wardrobe rut? Socks can be a colorful solution. They're also addictive—we bet you can't stop after just one pair! Whether quick knits or exquisitely detailed, these socks will have your feet (and style quota) covered.

Just Socks features both knit and crochet patterns for all levels of expertise, as well as patterns for men, women, and children. Colorwork, cables, lace, and plenty of luxurious yarns make it easy to create the most diverse sock drawer in town.

There are five chapters in this book, each focusing on a particular technique or type of sock. New knitters or crocheters will want to start in the beginning and work their way to the back, where reversible cables and stranded colorwork await. If you know the basics of sock knitting, feel free to jump around. (After knitting some of these socks, you'll want to jump around anyway.)

We assume you know the basic knitting skills of knit and purl and the basic crochet skills of single crochet, double crochet, and half double crochet. If you need to learn these basic stitches or refresh your memory, check out online tutorial sites such as the Craft Yarn Council of America's learntoknit.com or learntocrochet.com. You can also ask questions on the Council online forum at craftyarncouncil.com/cyca-forum. Libraries are also great offline resources, featuring many basic how-to books.

This book follows the standards and guidelines established by the Craft Yarn Council of America to help you choose patterns appropriate for your skill level. Each pattern is labeled as beginner, easy, intermediate, or experienced. **Beginner** patterns are suitable for first-time knitters and crocheters, requiring only basic stitch skills. **Easy** patterns call for basic stitches, repetitive pattern work, and simple color changes, and simple shaping and finishing. **Intermediate** patterns include a variety of stitches and techniques such as lacework, and simple intarsia. Normally, using double-pointed needles would fall into the intermediate skill category, but since most sock patterns call for them, we consider them a basic skill for the patterns in this book. Projects that use advanced techniques (including short rows, multicolor changes, complex cables or lace patterns), detailed shaping or finishing, or extremely fine-weight yarn are for **experienced** knitters and crocheters. The skill rating for each pattern is listed underneath its title.

KNOW YOUR YARNS

Socks can be made with almost any yarn. Thicker yarns (such as worsted or heavy worsted) are better for slipper socks and other cozy, warm footwear meant to be worn alone. Most socks are made with lighter weight yarn or sock yarn, though novelty and multi-textured yarns can be added for extra color and dimension. Knowing about the qualities of different yarn types can help you create all-new texture combinations in even the plainest sock pattern.

Traditional smooth yarns give excellent stitch definition and are perfect for cables and fancy stitch patterns. They range in weight and fiber content: everything from 100 percent wool to wool blends, high-tech microfibers, and cashmere. If you are a beginning sock knitter, stick to smoother yarns. It may be extra difficult to see your stitches with furry or fuzzy yarns at first. In time, you'll be able to make socks using just about any fiber you like!

YARN WEIGHTS

Knitters and crocheters can obtain different gauges working with the exact same needles, hooks, and yarn as someone else. Is it any wonder that they also describe yarn weights differently? The Craft Yarn Council of America has established a set of guidelines called the Standard Yarn Weight System to standardize descriptions of yarn thickness. The materials section of

STANDARD YARN WEIGHT SYSTEM

YARN WEIGHT SYMBOL & CATEGORY NAMES	1 SUPER FINE	2 FINE	3 LIGHT	4 MEDIUM	5 BULKY	6 SUPER BULKY
TYPE OF YARNS IN CATEGORY	Sock, Fingering, Baby	Sport, Baby	DK, Light Worsted	Worsted, Afghan, Aran	Chunky, Craft, Rug	Bulky, Roving
KNIT GAUGE RANGE* IN STOCKINETTE STITCH TO 4 INCHES	27–32 sts	23–26 sts	21–24 sts	16–20 sts	12–15 sts	6–11 sts
RECOMMENDED NEEDLE IN METRIC SIZE RANGE	2.25–3.25 mm	3.25–3.75 mm	3.75–4. 5mm	4.5–5.5 mm	5.5–8 mm	8 mm and larger
RECOMMENDED NEEDLE IN U.S. SIZE RANGE	1 to 3	3 to 5	5 to 7	7 to 9	9 to 11	11 and larger
CROCHET GAUGE RANGES* IN SINGLE CROCHET TO 4 INCHES	21–32 sts	16–20 sts	12–17 sts	11–14 sts	8–11 sts	5–9 sts
RECOMMENDED HOOK IN METRIC SIZE RANGE	2.25–3.5 mm	3.5–4.5 mm	4.5–5.5 mm	5.5–6.5 mm	6.5–9 mm	9 mm and larger
RECOMMENDED HOOK IN U.S. SIZE RANGE	B-1 to E4	E-4 to 7	7 to I-9	I-9 to K-10½	K-10½ to M-13	M-13 and larger

*Guidelines only: The above ranges reflect the most commonly used gauges and needle or hook sizes for specific yarn categories.

each pattern in this book features an icon of a skein of yarn with a number on it. That number corresponds to one of these standards. In this system, the smaller the number, the thinner the yarn. Check the chart on the previous page for suggested needle sizes and other information about using each yarn. If your gauge does not match the suggested pattern gauge exactly, try a needle or hook size larger or smaller.

SUBSTITUTING YARNS

All the socks featured in this book were made using Lion Brand yarn. If you want to substitute another yarn brand, select something of similar fiber content and weight. Many yarn brands also use the Standard Yarn Weight System on page 9. If your substitute yarn is the same weight as the one used in the pattern, chances are you will be able to make it work, although you may need to adjust your needle or hook size to obtain the correct gauge.

FINDING YOUR GAUGE

Determining your personal gauge may be a new concept if you haven't been knitting very long, but even if you have been knitting for years, a gauge swatch is crucial for sock knitting. A 1" (2.5 cm) difference in a sweater's width may be unnoticeable; in a sock, it's huge! Gauge, sometimes called *tension*, is the number of stitches and rows measured over a number of inches or centimeters of your knit fabric. As mentioned above, knitters and crocheters can vary in gauge even when using the exact same needles or hook.

To find your gauge, you will need to knit or crochet a swatch in the yarn and stitch listed in the pattern. It needs to be at least 4" x 4" (10 x 10 cm) for maximum accuracy. Using a ruler, but without pressing down on the swatch (which can distort the measurement), count the number of stitches in one 4" (10 cm) width, including half-stitches, if applicable. Repeat on more than one row of stitches, and average the numbers you obtain. This is where having a sizable gauge swatch comes in handy! If you are not close to (within half a stitch of) the pattern's recommended gauge, go up a needle size if your gauge is too small or go down a needle size if it's too big. Again, with socks, proper gauge can mean the difference between a child-sized sock and one that fits an adult! Take the time to swatch, and adjust your needle or hook size accordingly.

NEEDLES AND HOOKS

There are many different types of needles and hooks out there: metal, bamboo, wood, plastic—use whatever you like best! Many sock knitters choose metal double-pointed needles for their sturdiness and ultra-pointy tips (useful when working with ultrafine yarns). However, your preferences may vary based on the yarn you're using. Some slippery yarns are easier to work on bamboo or wooden needles, for example. If you are having a tough time working a certain yarn, try a different type of needle.

OTHER TOOLS

Each project will list additional tools and notions needed (such as cable needles or stitch markers). For all patterns, however, you should keep scissors; large-eyed, blunt needles (for weaving in ends); and a tape measure on hand.

SIZING

This can't be said too many times! Sizing is critical with socks, since an inch of difference can seem more like a mile. The Craft Yarn Council has developed a set of standard clothing sizes for knit and crocheted apparel, available online at yarnstandards.com, but socks are not covered. Be sure to measure your feet or a pair of socks that fit well to determine your measurements.

SOCKS FOR KIDS

Natural fibers such as wool and wool blends are generally the most durable for children's socks. If you have hardwood or other slippery floors in your home, though, you may want to add some traction to hand-knit house slippers. Many yarn shops sell leather soles you can sew to the bottoms of your slippers.

EXTRA DURABILITY

A handknit or hand-crocheted sweater can last for generations; handknit socks are less forgiving. Fortunately, there is a solution. Wooly nylon is a sewing notion often used by sock knitters to give more durability to the heels and toes of their socks. By using it as a carry-along yarn (one that is held along with the main yarn as you knit), you'll get much more wear out of your precious handmade socks.

Although hand washing your socks is the best way to guarantee they'll last a long, long time, you can also wash most socks in your machine on the delicate cycle with cold water. Put them in a lingerie bag for easy retrieval after the spin cycle, and stretch them over sock drying frames for maximum longevity. These sock drying frames, available from knitting catalogs and many yarn shops, will help your socks dry without shrinking or stretching and keep them looking their best.

TECHNIQUES AND FINISHING

Single-color socks have very little finishing: Tuck in a few ends and you're done! But there are some finer points to address, and techniques you'll use again and again, and not only in socks!

Casting On to Double-Pointed Needles When knitting in the round on double-pointed needles, it is often easier to cast the required number of stitches onto one longer needle, then divide the stitches among three or four needles according to the directions (most patterns will specify how many stitches to put on each needle; if there is no number given, divide the cast-on number equally).

Grafting/Kitchener Stitch Used to join two pieces of knitting, Kitchener stitch is most often used at the bottom of a sock at the toe. Hold both needles parallel with your end thread coming off the back needle. Place end through the tapestry needle as if to sew. Go up through the first stitch on the back needle as if to knit, leaving stitch on the needle. This locks the stitch. Go to the front needle and go through the first stitch as if to purl, leaving stitch on the needle. This locks that stitch.

Repeat the following steps enclosed with asterisks until all stitches are removed from both needles, making a smooth seam in the toe of the sock. Remember to purl, purl; knit, knit as you move back and forth between the needles. Thinking through the process step by step helps make the Kitchener stitch easier to execute.

**Next, go to the back needle and go through first stitch as if to purl, dropping stitch off the needle. Go through next stitch on back needle as if to knit, leaving the stitch on the needle.

Move to the front needle and go through first stitch as if to knit, dropping stitch off the needle. Go through next stitch on front needle as if to purl, leaving the stitch on the needle.**

Magic-Loop Method The so-called Magic Loop method is a way to knit a small tube, such as a sock, on one long circular needle. Since sock knitting is essentially the art of making small tubes, this method is perfect for knitters who don't like using double-pointed needles. Cast on the required number of stitches onto the circular needle (which can be anywhere from 16" to 40" (40 to 101 cm) long, but 24" (61 cm) is a good length for most socks). At the center of the cast-on stitches, pull the extra cord length out, drawing the cast-on ends out to the pointy needle tips. Join the round, and begin to knit as directed. When you knit almost all the stitches on one needle off to the other, readjust your cord by pulling it out the new center of the stitches. Continue knitting additional rounds as the pattern directs.

Two-Circular-Needles Method This method is slightly similar to Magic Loop in that you are using only the active sides of the needles to work around your tube, leaving the unused side to hang out the end of your stitches. Cast the required number of stitches onto one circular needle, then put half of them onto a second circular needle and join the round. You can use two circular needles of any length, though 16" to 24" (40 to 61 cm) needles are optimal (the more extra cord, the longer it will take you to pull that extra through the stitches when getting ready to switch needles). Knit across the back needle with the right-hand side of the front needle. Turn the work and knit across what is now the back needle. Repeat.

1.

SWEET AND SIMPLE

These patterns may look complex, but they are all rewarding beginner projects that use basic knit and purl stitches or single and double crochet to get you started on the road to sock success.

JOAN'S KNITTED SOCKS

DESIGNED BY LION BRAND YARN

KNIT/BEGINNER

These knitted socks are basic yet versatile, perfect for testing your sock-making skills!

SIZE

Women's S (M)

Sample shown 8" long x 7" around ball of foot (20.3 cm x 17.8 cm).

MATERIALS

 LION BRAND® LION® WOOL

100% WOOL

3 OZ (85 G) 158 YD (144 M) BALL

2 balls #133 Pumpkin, or color of your choice

- Double-pointed needles sizes 6 + 8 (4 + 5 mm) [sizes 7 + 9 (4.5 + 5.5 mm)], *or size to obtain gauge*

GAUGE

For S 4 stitches and 6 rows = 1" (2.5 cm) with size 8 needles.
For M 4 stitches and 6 rows = 1" (2.5 cm) with size 9 needles.
Be sure to check your gauge.

NOTES

Work with 2 strands of yarn held together throughout.

The length of the leg can be made longer by knitting the leg section 1–2" (2.5–5 cm) longer.

RIBBING

With size 6 (7) double-pointed needles, cast on 32 stitches (divided as follows: 10 stitches on needle 1, 12 stitches on needle 2, 10 stitches on needle 3). Join, work around in knit 1, purl 1 rib for 12 rounds.

LEG

Change to size 8 (9) double-pointed needles. Work in stockinette stitch (knit every round) until piece measures 6" (15 cm).

HEEL

Next round Knit 8, put remaining stitches on needle 2, turn.

Next row Slip 1, purl 7 plus 8 more stitches from needle 3. Divide instep stitches evenly on 2 double-pointed needles to be worked later. Work heel flap in stockinette stitch for about 2" (5 cm) always slipping first stitch of each row, ending with a right side row. Note: You should have 7 loops along the sides (1 loop for every 2 rows).

TURN HEEL

Row 1 Slip 1, purl 8, purl 2 stitches together, purl 1, turn.
Row 2 Slip 1, knit 3, slip 1, knit 1, pass slipped stitch over, knit 1, turn.
Row 3 Slip 1, purl 4, purl 2 stitches together, purl 1, turn.
Row 4 Slip 1, knit 5, slip 1, knit 1, pass slipped stitch over, knit 1, turn.
Row 5 Slip 1, purl 6, purl 2 stitches together, purl 1, turn.
Row 6 Slip 1, knit 7, slip 1, knit 1, pass slipped stitch over, knit 1, do not turn—10 stitches remaining.

Round 1 Pick up and knit 7 stitches along side of heel plus 1 stitch at the intersection of the needles. Knit across instep stitches onto one needle. Pick up and knit 1 stitch at intersection at other side plus 7 stitches along edge, plus knit 5 stitches from heel onto same needle. Note: Beginning of round should be at center of heel. Place the stitches that you picked up at intersections on the instep needle.

Round 2 Needle 1: Knit. Needle 2: Slip 1, knit 1, pass the slipped stitch over, knit to two stitches from end, knit 2 stitches together (this prevents a hole that may form at this place). Needle 3: Knit.

GUSSET

Round 1 Knit to within 3 stitches of end of needle 1, knit 2 stitches together, knit 1; on needle 2, knit across, on needle 3, knit 1, slip 1, knit 1, pass slipped stitch over, knit to end.

Round 2 Knit.

Repeat last 2 rounds until 32 stitches remain. Work even in stockinette stitch to desired length, leaving about 1–2" (4–5 cm) for toe shaping. (Note: For size 7 shoe, knit to 7" [20 cm] from back of heel before starting toe shaping.)

TOE

Round 1 Knit to within 3 stitches of end of needle 1, knit 2 stitches together, knit 1; on needle 2, knit 1, slip 1, knit 1, pass slipped stitch over, knit to within 3 stitches of end, knit 2 stitches together, knit 1; on needle 3, knit 1, knit 2 stitches together, knit to end.

Round 2 Knit.

Repeat last 2 rounds until 16 stitches remain. Knit first 4 stitches of last round with needle 3, and weave these 8 stitches to 8 stitches on instep needle using Kitchener stitch (pages 11–12).

JOAN'S CROCHETED SOCKS

DESIGNED BY LION BRAND YARN
CROCHET/BEGINNER

These crocheted socks, like their knitted cousins, are basic yet versatile and a great opportunity to practice your crochet skills!

SIZE

Women's S (M)
Sample shown 10" long x 8.5" around ball of foot (25 cm x 21.5 cm)

MATERIALS

 LION BRAND® LION® WOOL
100% WOOL
3 OZ (85 G) 158 YD (144 M) BALL

2 balls #113 Scarlet, or color of your choice

• Crochet hooks sizes G-6 and H-8 (4 and 5 mm) [sizes H-8 and I-9 (5 and 5.5 mm)], *or size to obtain gauge*
• large-eyed, blunt needle

GAUGE

For S 5 single crochet = 1" (2.5 cm) with size H-8 (5 mm) hook.
For M 4 single crochet = 1" (2.5 cm) with size I-9 (5.5 mm) hook.

Be sure to check your gauge.

NOTES

These socks are easy to make in one flat piece. When finished, they will resemble Turkish knitted socks, with the heel appearing to stick out when folded. On the foot, however, they fit exactly as a commercial sock.

The leg can be made longer by crocheting the leg section an inch or two (2.5–5 cm) longer. The length of the foot can also be increased, ensuring that the top and bottom of the foot are the same length.

RIBBING

With smaller hook, chain 11.
Row 1 Single crochet in 2nd chain from hook, single crochet in each chain across, turn—10 single crochet.
Row 1 Chain 1, working in back loops only, single crochet in each single crochet across, turn—10 single crochet.
Repeat row 2 for 40 more rows. Do not turn. Working along side of ribbing, work 1 single crochet in each row, turn—40 single crochet.

LEG

With larger hook, work back and forth in single crochet, working through both loops, on 40 stitches until piece measures 7" (18 cm) from beginning of sock. Cut yarn.

TOP OF FOOT

Row 1 With right side facing and larger hook, join yarn in 11th stitch from edge, chain 1, single crochet in same stitch, single crochet in each of next 19 single crochet, turn.
Row 2 Chain 1, single crochet in each single crochet across. Turn—20 single crochet.

Repeat row 2 until piece measures 6" (15 cm) above joining or desired length, allowing 2" (5 cm) for toe, ending on wrong side. Note: The heel will add another 2" (5 cm). Measure foot and subtract 4" (10 cm) total for heel and toe to determine desired length.

TOP OF TOE

*Row 1 Chain 1, decrease 1 single crochet in next 2 single crochet, single crochet across to within last 2 single crochet, decrease 1 stitch in next 2 single crochet, turn.

Row 2 Chain 1, work even in single crochet, turn. Repeat last 2 rows until 10 single crochet remain, ending with row 2.

BOTTOM OF TOE

Row 1 Chain 1, 2 single crochet in first single crochet, single crochet across to last single crochet, 2 single crochet in last single crochet, turn.

Row 2 Chain 1, work even in single crochet, turn. Repeat last 2 rows until there are 20 single crochet.*

BOTTOM OF FOOT

Work even on 20 single crochet until piece measure 6" (15 cm) or same length as straight portion of foot.

HEEL

Repeat from * to * as for toe shaping. Fasten off.

FINISHING

Sew back leg seam. Fold sock in middle of the toe and sew both sides of foot. Fold the heel in half, as with toe, and sew sides. Position the heel piece so that center of heel is in line with leg seam, and sew.

TRAVELING SOCK

DESIGNED BY BETH SKWARECKI

KNIT/BEGINNER

This simple sock is an ideal first sock for beginners. Experienced knitters may find it an excellent project to knit on vacation, since it requires very little attention.

SIZE

Women's M (Men's L)
Length is adjustable.
Sample shown: 9½" long x 7" around ball of foot (24.1 x 17.8 cm)

MATERIALS

 LION BRAND® LION® WOOL
100% WOOL
3 OZ (85 G) 197 YD (180 M) BALL

1 ball each #188 Paprika (A) and #129 Cocoa (B), or colors of your choice

- 1 set size 5 (3.75 mm) double-pointed needles, *or size to obtain gauge*
- Large-eyed, blunt needle
- 2 stitch markers

GAUGE

22 sts + 26 rows = 4" (10 cm) in stockinette stitch.
Be sure to check your gauge.

NOTES

When you come to the heel, you will insert a contrasting scrap of yarn. If you prefer, you can skip this step, and later, instead of removing the scrap, cut a strand of yarn where you want the heel to go.

CUFF

With A, loosely cast on 36 (48) stitches.
[Knit 1, purl 1] for 7 rows. This creates a stretchy ribbing to hold the sock up.
Knit 35 (47) rows in stockinette stitch.

PLACEHOLDER FOR HEEL

With B, knit 18 (24) stitches.
Break the B yarn.
Slip B stitches from your right needle back to the left needle, and return to the point where you stopped knitting with A. Continue by knitting all stitches (including the B ones you just made) with A yarn. This produces a thin stripe of B across half your sock.

FOOT

With A, work 35 (47) rows, or until foot is desired length. On last row, place two markers, one at the beginning of the round and one 18 (24) stitches later. If you try the sock on, these markers will be on either side of your foot, at your pinky and big toe.

TOE
Change to B yarn.

Row 1 (Knit 2 stitches together, knit until 2 stitches before marker, slip slip knit) twice.

Row 2 Knit 1 row.

Repeat these 2 rows until only 12 (16) stitches remain.

Seam the toe with Kitchener stitch.

HEEL
Carefully remove the scrap of B yarn. Put the resulting 35 (47) stitches on your needles. Place markers at either side of the heel.

Row 1 Knit 16 (22), slip slip knit, knit 14 (20), slip slip knit.

Row 2 Knit 1 row.

Repeat these 2 rows until only 12 (16) stitches remain. Seam the heel with Kitchener stitch.

STRIPED FOOTIES

DESIGNED BY AMY POPE
KNIT/BEGINNER

Knitting worsted yarn at 6 stitches per inch instead of 4 makes for long-lasting and better-wearing socks. The dense fabric will keep your feet extra warm in wintertime. Try them out as house socks! If you don't want to use Kitchener stitch, you can keep decreasing until only 2 stitches remain on each needle, and then break yarn, run the yarn tail through the remaining stitches twice, and sew up the gaps.

SIZE

Women's L
Sample shown 10" long x 8.5"
around ball of foot (25 x 21.5 cm)

MATERIALS

 LION BRAND® LION® WOOL
100% WOOL
3 OZ (85 G) 158 YD (144 M) BALL

1 ball each #147 Purple (A), #132 Lemongrass (B), or colors of your choice

- Smooth waste yarn in a contrasting color
- Set of 5 size 3 (3.25 mm) double-pointed needles, *or size to obtain gauge*

- Stitch markers
- Large-eyed, blunt needle

GAUGE

24 stitches + 36 rows = 4" (10 cm).
Be sure to check your gauge.

NOTE

These socks are striped in a 6-row repeat with an afterthought heel.

CUFF

With A, cast on 44 stitches. Join, being careful not to twist, and place marker to indicate beginning of round. Distribute stitches so that there are 11 stitches per needle. Work in knit 2, purl 2 rib for 4 rows.

Rows 5–6 Work in stockinette.

Rows 7–9 Switch to B. Knit 3 rows.

PLACE HEEL

Row 10 Knit across 22 stitches using waste yarn. You will be coming back later to "unzip" these stitches and work the heel. After knitting in waste yarn, return to beginning of round and knit across the placeholder stitches with B.

Rows 12–13 Knit with B before switching back to A.

FOOT

Continue knitting foot, alternating colors every 6 rounds, until sock measures approximately 1¾" (4.5 cm) shorter than the intended length from the waste yarn to the end. (Sample shows 4 full stripes of each color.)

SHAPE TOE

Round 1 On needle 1, knit 1, slip slip knit, knit across. On needle 2, knit to last 3 stitches, knit 2 stitches together, knit 1. On needle 3, knit 1, slip slip knit, knit across. On needle 4, knit to last 3 stitches, knit 2 stitches together, knit 1.

Round 2 Knit to end of round. Using A, alternate these 2 rounds until there are 6 stitches on each needle, and then repeat round 1 only until only 3 stitches remain on each needle.

Graft remaining stitches using Kitchener stitch.

HEEL

Round 1 Using 4 needles and distributing stitches evenly, carefully pick up each stitch above and below your waste yarn. There will be one more stitch on one side than the other. Pick out the waste yarn row. You should now have 2 needles with stitches above and below a long hole in your knitting. Beginning with B, knit all stitches, picking up and knitting 2 stitches in each gap at the ends of the slit.

Round 2 Decrease evenly around to bring your stitch count to 48 stitches. Arrange stitches so that there are 12 stitches on each needle, and the side corners of the heel line up evenly with the sides of the toe.

Round 3 Knit to end of round.

Round 4 Switch to A. On needle 1, knit 1, slip slip knit, knit across. On needle 2, knit to last 3 stitches, knit 2 stitches together, knit 1. On needle 3, knit 1, slip slip knit, knit across. On needle 4, knit to last 3 stitches, knit 2 stitches together, knit 1.

Rounds 5–6 Knit.

Continue working these 2 decrease rounds until 24 stitches remain, and then repeat rounds 4 and 5 until 16 stitches remain. Graft the final 16 stitches using Kitchener stitch.

Weave in ends, wash, and block.

TOE-UP STRIPED SLIPPER SOCKS

DESIGNED BY ANASTACIA E. ZITTEL

CROCHET/INTERMEDIATE

These striped slipper-style socks are quick to crochet and fun to wear, around the house or anywhere else you need a little excitement.

SIZE

Women's M

Sample shown 9" long x 7" around ball of foot (22.9 x 17.8 cm)

MATERIALS

 LION BRAND® MICROSPUN
100% MICROFIBER ACRYLIC
2½ OZ (70 G) 168 YD (154 M) BALL

1 ball each #124 Mocha (A) and #126 Coffee (B), or colors of your choice

- Size E-4 (3.5 mm) crochet hook, *or size to obtain gauge*
- Large-eyed, blunt needle

GAUGE

44 single crochet + 10 rows = 4" (10 cm).

Be sure to check your gauge.

NOTE

Adjustable Loop Make a large loop by putting the yarn tail behind the working yarn (yarn coming from the skein), leaving a long tail. With your hook, draw the working yarn through the loop so you have one loop on the hook, and follow the first round working over and into the ring. At the end of the first round, pull the yarn tail to close the ring. This gives you a seamless, no-hole beginning to anything you crochet. Work in rounds unless otherwise stated, and join rounds at the end of every row. For color changes, either carry the unused color along the seam or fasten off at the end of each color change and weave in ends.

STITCH EXPLANATIONS

Single Crochet Decrease Insert hook into stitch indicated, yarn over hook and pull yarn through, insert hook into next stitch indicated, yarn over hook and pull yarn through, yarn over hook and pull yarn through all loops on hook.

Front Post Double Crochet Yarn over, insert hook from front to back to front around post of stitch indicated, draw up loop, (yarn over, draw through 2 loops on hook) twice. Skip stitch behind front post double crochet on working row.

Back Post Double Crochet Yarn over, insert hook from back to front to back around post of stitch indicated, draw up loop, (yarn over, draw through 2 loops on hook) twice. Skip stitch behind back post double crochet on working row.

BODY

Starting with toe and A, make an adjustable loop.

Round 1 Chain 1, 6 single crochet into adjustable loop. Join with slip stitch in first single crochet. Pull tail end tight to close—6 single crochet.

Round 2 Chain 1, 2 single crochet in each single crochet around. Join with slip stitch in first single crochet—12 single crochet.

Round 3 Chain 1, 2 single crochet in first single crochet, single crochet in next single crochet, *2 single crochet in next single crochet, single crochet in next single crochet; repeat from * around. Join with slip stitch in first single crochet—18 single crochet.

Round 4 Chain 1, 2 single crochet in first single crochet, single crochet in each of next 2 single crochet, *2 single crochet in next single crochet, single crochet in each of next 2 single crochet; repeat from * around. Join with slip stitch in first single crochet—24 single crochet.

Round 5 Chain 1, 2 single crochet in first single crochet, single crochet in each of next 3 single crochet, *2 single crochet in next single crochet, single crochet in each of next 3 single crochet; repeat from * around. Join with slip stitch in first single crochet—30 single crochet.

Round 6 Chain 1, 2 single crochet in first single crochet, single crochet in each of next 4 single crochet, *2 single crochet in next single crochet, single crochet in each of next 4 single crochet; repeat from * around. Join with slip stitch in first single crochet—36 single crochet.

Round 7 Join Color B in any single crochet, chain 1, single crochet in each single crochet around. Join with slip stitch in first single crochet.

Rounds 8–10 Chain 1, single crochet in each single crochet around. Join with slip stitch in first single crochet.

Rounds 11–14 Join A, chain 1, single crochet in each single crochet around. Join with slip stitch in first single crochet.

Rounds 15–38 Repeat rounds 7–14, alternating colors every 4 rows as established, and ending last 4 rows with A.

Rounds 39–40 With B, chain 1, single crochet in each single crochet around. Join with slip stitch in first single crochet.

SET UP AFTERTHOUGHT HEEL

Round 41 Chain 18, skip next 18 single crochet, single crochet in each single crochet to end. Join with slip stitch in first single crochet—18 single crochet + 18 chain.

Round 42 Chain 1, single crochet in each of next 18 chain stitches, single crochet in each of next 18 single crochet. Join with slip stitch in first single crochet—36 single crochet.

Rounds 43–46 With A, chain 1, single crochet in each single crochet around. Join with slip stitch in first single crochet.

Rounds 47–50 With B, single crochet in each single crochet around. Join with slip stitch in first single crochet. Fasten off B.

CUFF

Round 1 Chain 3, double crochet in next single crochet and in each single crochet around. Join with

slip stitch in 3rd chain of beginning chain—26 double crochet.

Round 2 Work front post double crochet in first stitch, *back post double crochet in next stitch, front post double crochet in next stitch; repeat from * around. Join with slip stitch in first front post double crochet.

Rounds 3–4 Work front post double crochet in each front post double crochet, and back post double crochet in each back post double crochet. Fasten off.

Using large-eyed, blunt needle, weave in tail ends.

AFTERTHOUGHT HEEL

With A, join yarn in the remaining loop of any chain you made for the heel in Round 42.

Round 1 Chain 1, single crochet in same stitch, single crochet in each of next 17 chain, working around other side of heel, single crochet in each of next 18 single crochet. Join with slip stitch in first single crochet—36 single crochet.

Round 2 Chain 1, single crochet in each single crochet around. Join with slip stitch in first single crochet.

Round 3 Chain 1, single crochet decrease over first 2 single crochet, single crochet in each of next 16 single crochet, single crochet decrease over next 2 single crochet, single crochet in each of last 16 single crochet. Join with slip stitch in first single crochet— 34 single crochet.

Round 4 Chain 1, single crochet decrease over first 2 single crochet, single crochet in each of next 15 single crochet, single crochet decrease over next 2 single crochet, single crochet in each of last 15 single crochet—32 single crochet.

Round 5 Chain 1, single crochet decrease over first 2 single crochet, single crochet in each of next 14 single crochet, single crochet decrease over next 2 single crochet, single crochet in each of last 14 single crochet. Join with slip stitch in first single crochet— 30 single crochet.

Continue decreasing each round by 2 single crochet until you have 12 stitches remaining.

Fasten off, leaving a long tail. Using large-eyed, blunt needle, carefully weave tail end through remaining single crochet and sew to close.

HIKING SOCKS

DESIGNED BY NATASHA FIALKOV
KNIT/EASY

These instructions are written using the Magic Loop method (see page 12) but can easily be adapted for two circular needles or double-pointed needles. Sometimes you need a little color on your feet, and these socks deliver! Who says sporty socks have to be plain?

SIZE

Women's S
Sample shown 8" long x 7" around ball of foot (20.3 cm x 17.8 cm)

MATERIALS

 LION BRAND® LION® WOOL
100% WOOL
3 OZ (85 G) 158 YD (144 M) BALL

2 balls #147 Purple, or color of your choice

- 1 size 6 (4 mm) 36" (91 cm) circular needle, *or size to obtain gauge*
- Large-eyed, blunt needle
- Stitch markers

GAUGE

16 stitches + 24 rows = 4" (10 cm). *Be sure to check your gauge.*

NOTES

Designer used a knit 2, purl 2 rib for the entire sock. If you like, you may continue the pattern on the foot, or just end it at the ankle.

CUFF

Cast on 40 stitches. Join in the round, making sure not to twist. Work in knit 2, purl 2 rib for 5" (13 cm) or desired cuff length. Divide stitches in half, and reserve 20 instep stitches on the cable of the circular needle.

HEEL FLAP

Work 20 heel stitches back and forth on one needle:
Row 1 Slip 1 as if to purl, *knit 1, slip 1 as if to knit; repeat from * to 1 stitch from end of row, knit 1.
Row 2 Slip 1 as if to purl, purl 18, knit 1.

Repeat last 2 rows 14 times or for about 2¼" (6 cm), ending with a right side row.

TURN HEEL

Row 1 (WS) Slip 1, purl 10, purl 2 stitches together, purl 1, turn.
Row 2 Slip 1, knit 3, slip slip knit, knit 1, turn.
Row 3 Slip 1, purl to 1 stitch from gap, purl 2 stitches together (closing gap), purl 1, turn.
Row 4 Slip 1, knit to 1 stitch from gap, slip slip knit, knit 1, turn.
Repeat rows 3 and 4 until 10 stitches remain, ending with a knit row.

GUSSET

With right side facing, pick up 10 stitches at side of heel flap, then pick up 2 more.
At top of gusset, place marker, work 20 instep stitches in ribbing

pattern, place marker, pick up
2 stitches.

At top of gusset, pick up 10 stitches
from other side of heel flap, knit 10
heel stitches, place marker.
Arrange stitches on the needles
and cord so that the sock is divided
in left and right halves. The center
of the instep is the beginning of
the round.
Work stitches as they appear for 1
round, knitting together the two
stitches picked up at the top of

each gusset to prevent a gap from
forming.
Round 1 Knit to first marker, slip
marker, slip slip knit, work stitches
in pattern to 2 stitches before
second marker, knit 2 stitches
together, knit to end of round.
Round 2 Knit to first marker, slip
marker, knit 1, slip slip knit, work
to 3 stitches before second marker,
knit 2 stitches together, knit 1, slip
marker, knit to end of round.
Round 3 Knit.

Repeat rounds 2 and 3 until 40
stitches remain.

FOOT
Work in pattern or stockinette
stitch to about 2" (5 cm) shorter
than the length of your foot. Try the
sock on to check the length, if
needed. Remove markers.

TOE
Knit 10 stitches, place marker. This
is the new beginning of the round.
Round 1 Knit 1, slip slip knit, rib 14,
knit 2 stitches together, knit 1, place
marker, knit 1, slip slip knit, rib 14,
knit 2 stitches together, knit 1.
Round 2 Work in ribbing.
Round 3 Knit 1, slip slip knit, rib to
3 stitches before second marker,
knit 2 stitches together, knit 1, slip
marker, slip slip knit, rib to 3
stitches from end of round, knit 2
stitches together, knit 1.
Repeat rows 2 and 3 until 14
stitches remain.

FINISHING
Graft remaining stitches with
Kitchener stitch. Weave in ends
and block.

AMISH APRÈS-SKI SOCKS

DESIGNED BY NATASHA FIALKOV
KNIT/BEGINNER

The instructions are written using two circular needles, but can easily be modified for one circular needle or double-pointed needles (see pages 11 and 12).

SIZE

Women's S/M
Sample shown: 9" long x 8" around ball of foot (22.9 cm x 20.3 cm)

MATERIALS

 LION BRAND® HOMESPUN®
98% ACRYLIC, 2% POLYESTER
6 OZ (170 G) 185 YD (169 M) SKEIN

1 skein #395 Meadow, or color of your choice

- 2 size 10 (6 mm) 36" (91 cm) circular needles, *or size to obtain gauge*
- Stitch markers
- Large-eyed, blunt needle

GAUGE

14 stitches + 20 rows = 4" (10 cm).
Be sure to check your gauge.

CUFF

Cast on 32 stitches. Divide stitches evenly onto 2 circular needles and join in the round, making sure not to twist.
Knit all rounds for 4–5" (10–13 cm) or 3" (7.5 cm) less than desired cuff length.
For a more fitted ankle (optional), work 1 round decreasing 4 stitches evenly.
Knit all rounds to desired length (about 3" [7.5 cm]).

HEEL FLAP

Work half the stitches (14) back and forth on one needle as follows:
Row 1 Slip 1 as if to purl, *knit 1, slip 1 as if to knit; repeat from * to 1 stitch from end, knit 1.
Row 2 Slip 1 as if to purl, purl 12, knit 1.
Repeat the last 2 rows 14 times (about 2½" [5.75 cm]), ending with a right side row.

TURN HEEL

Row 1 (WS) Slip 1, purl 7, purl 2 stitches together, purl 1, turn.
Row 2 Slip 1, knit 2, slip slip knit, knit 1, turn.
Row 3 Slip 1, purl to 1 stitch from gap, purl 2 stitches together (closing gap), purl 1, turn.
Row 4 Slip 1, knit to 1 stitch from gap, slip slip knit, knit 1, turn.
Repeat last 2 rows until 7 stitches remain, ending with a right side row.

GUSSET

Needle 1 is now beginning of round.
Continuing with needle 1 (right side): Pick up 6 stitches from side of heel flap, pick up 2 more at side of gusset, place marker, knit 7

instep stitches. Needle 2: Knit 7 instep stitches, place marker, pick up 2 stitches at top of gusset, pick up 6 stitches from other side of heel flap, knit 7 heel flap stitches. (Sock is now divided into left and right halves on the needles, with the row beginning in the center of the instep.)

Work 1 round, making sure to knit together the 2 stitches at the top of each gusset to prevent a gap from forming.

Round 1 Needle 1: Knit to marker, slip marker, slip slip knit, knit to end. Needle 2: Knit to 2 stitches before marker, knit 2 stitches together, knit to end.

Round 2 Needle 1: Knit to marker, slip marker, knit 1, slip slip knit, knit to end. Needle 2: Knit to 3 stitches before marker, knit 2 stitches together, knit 1, slip marker.

Round 3 Knit.

Repeat rows 2 and 3 until 28 stitches remain.

Knit 7 rounds or to about 2" (5 cm) shorter than the length of your foot, trying sock on to check the length if desired. Remove markers.

TOE

Round 1 Knit 7, place marker (this marks the beginning of the sole stitches and the new beginning of the round), knit 1, slip slip knit, knit 8, knit 2 stitches together, knit 1, place marker, knit 1, slip slip knit, knit 8, knit 2 stitches together, knit 1.

Round 2 Knit.

Round 3 Knit 1, slip slip knit, knit to 3 stitches before second marker, knit 2 stitches together, knit 1, slip marker, slip slip knit, knit to 3 stitches from end of round, knit 2 stitches together, knit 1. Repeat rows 2 and 3 until 14 stitches remain.

FINISHING

Graft remaining stitches with Kitchener stitch. Weave in ends and block.

2.
CABLES
AND LACE

This chapter focuses on the yin-yang relation-ship between cables and lace. Cabling produces a thicker and, therefore, warmer fabric, while lacy socks are more suited to warmer days. Making fancy socks is an excellent way to experiment with texture and technique, and work your way up to larger lace projects, if you like.

REVERSIBLE CABLE SOCK

DESIGNED BY BETH SKWARECKI
KNIT/INTERMEDIATE

This sock has cabled ribbing on both sides of the cuff, so you can show off the cables whether you wear the cuffs up or down. Try them in a bright color, as shown here, or in more muted tones—the reversible cable is gorgeous no matter what.

SIZE

Women's L (Men's L)
Sample shown 10" long x 10" around ball of foot (25.4 x 25.4 cm) You can adjust the length of the sock to fit.

MATERIALS

 LION BRAND® LION® WOOL
100% WOOL
3 OZ (85 G) 158 YD (144 M) BALL

1 (2) ball #187 Goldenrod, or color of your choice

- 1 set size 5 (3.75 mm) double-pointed needles, *or size to obtain gauge*
- Large-eyed, blunt needle
- 2 stitch markers

GAUGE

16 stitches + 24 rows = 4" (10 cm) in stockinette stitch.
Be sure to check your gauge.

STITCH EXPLANATIONS

t2k (Twist Two Knit Stitches) Knit the 2nd stitch on the needle, but do not remove it from your left needle; then knit the 1st stitch on the needle; then remove both stitches from the left needle.

t2p (Twist Two Purl Stitches) Purl the 2nd stitch on the needle, but do not remove it from your left needle; then purl the 1st stitch on the needle; then remove both stitches from the left needle.

CUFF

Cast on 40 (48) stitches. Join, being careful not to twist, and place marker to indicate beginning of round.

Round 1 *Knit 2, purl 2; repeat from * across.

Round 2 *Knit 2, purl 2, t2k, t2p; repeat from * across.

Round 3 *Knit 2, purl 2; repeat from * across.

Round 4 *Knit 2, purl 2; repeat from * across.

Repeat rows 1–4 seven more times. Knit 6 rows in stockinette stitch.

HEEL

Work short-row heel as follows:

Row 1 Knit 19 (23), wrap and turn.

Row 2 Purl 18 (22), wrap and turn.

Row 3 Knit 17 (21), wrap and turn.

Row 4 Purl 16 (20), wrap and turn.

Continue in this manner, working one fewer stitch each row. When only 6 (8) stitches remain live between the wrapped stitches, begin increasing as follows:

Row 1 Knit 6 (8), knit wrap together with next stitch, wrap and turn. (You now have 1 stitch with 2 wraps.)

Row 2 Purl 7 (9), purl wraps together with next stitch, wrap and turn.

Row 3 Knit 8 (10), knit wraps together with next stitch, wrap and turn.

Row 4 Purl 9 (11), purl wraps together with next stitch, wrap and turn.

Continue until no double-wrapped stitches remain. Knit 1 row without turning, knitting the 2 wrapped stitches with their wraps.

FOOT

Work 34 (47) rounds or until foot is desired length. On last row, place two markers: one at the beginning of the round, and one 20 (24) stitches later. If you try the sock on, these markers will be on either side of your foot, at your pinky and big toe.

TOE

Round 1 *Knit 2 stitches together, knit until 2 stitches before marker, slip slip knit; repeat from *.

Round 2 Knit 1 row.

Repeat these 2 rounds until only 14 (16) stitches remain.

FINISHING

Join the toes stitches with Kitchener stitch. Weave in ends and block.

LUCKY 7 SOCKS

DESIGNED BY MARTHA ONUSCONICH
KNIT/EXPERIENCED

These soft and elegant socks have a namesake with many of the same qualities: the designer's cat! They're a challenging knit but well worth it. Knit in seven pieces, they're also fully refootable. This is great since you'll want to wear them often!

SIZE
Women's L
Sample shown 10" long x 10½" around ball of foot (25.4 x 26.7 cm)

MATERIALS

 LION BRAND® MICROSPUN
100% MICROFIBER ACRYLIC
2½ OZ (70 G) 168 YD (154 M) BALL

2 balls #194 Lime, or color of your choice

- Set of 5 size 1 (2.25 mm) double-pointed needles, *or size to obtain gauge*
- Stitch markers
- Large-eyed, blunt needle

GAUGE
24 stitches and 32 rows = 4" (10 cm) in stockinette stitch.

Be sure to check your gauge.

STITCH EXPLANATIONS
Cross Left Knit second stitch on left needle through back of loop and leave on needle; knit first stitch and slip both stitches from left needle.
Cross Right Knit second stitch on left needle and leave on needle; knit first stitch and slip both stitches from left needle.
M1L (Left-Slanting Make-One Increase) With left needle and from the front, pick up yarn between last stitch worked and first stitch on left needle; knit the picked-up yarn through the back loop.
M1R (Right-Slanting Make-One Increase) With left needle and from the back, pick up yarn between last stitch worked and first stitch on left needle; knit through the front loop.

PICOT EDGING
Cast on 68 stitches using provisional cast-on. Divide the stitches among three double-pointed needles. Join in the round, being careful not to twist, and place marker to indicate beginning of round.

Rounds 1–6 Knit all stitches.
Round 7 *Knit 2 stitches together, yo, repeat from * around.
Rounds 8–15 Knit all stitches.
Fold cuff with wrong sides together, carefully pull out the provisional cast-on from about 20 stitches at a time and pick up freed stitches on a needle. Hold the freed stitches behind the live stitches and knit together 1 stitch from each edge. When all freed stitches from the needle are used, pull out more of the cast-on and repeat until both edges have been completely joined.

Place marker to indicate beginning of round.

RIBBING

Work knit 2, purl 2 ribbing for 1½" (4 cm), or roughly 15 rows.
Move marker 1 stitch to the left (between the first 2 knit stitches).
Setup row *Cross left, cross right, repeat from * around.

CUFF

Work following pattern until cuff is 7" (19 cm) or ½" (1.25 cm) less than desired length, ending with round 3.
Rounds 1–3 *Purl 1, knit 2, purl 1; repeat from * around.
Round 4 *Purl 1, cross right, purl 1; repeat from * around.
Setup for instep and heel/sole: purl 1, knit 34, purl 1 (these are the 36 instep stitches), place marker; knit 32 (heel/sole stitches).
For the next 4 rounds, continue working the instep stitches in the cuff pattern while working the heel stitches as follows:
Round 1 *Cross right, cross left, repeat from * to marker.
Round 2 (and all even rounds) Knit to marker.

Round 3 From this point, the instep and heel/sole are worked separately back and forth. The instep is worked first with the heel/sole stitches held in reserve. The heel/sole stitches are worked second and joined to the slipped-stitch edges of the already completed instep. The toe is worked in the round. Place all the instep stitches on a single needle and reserve the heel stitches on stitch holders or scrap yarn.

INSTEP

Row 1 (RS) Knit 1 tbl, *cross right, purl 2; repeat from * until 1 stitch remains, slip that stitch as if to purl with yarn in front.
Row 2 and all wrong side rows Knit 1 through back of loop, *purl 2, knit 2; repeat from * until 1 stitch remains, slip that stitch as if to purl with yarn in front.
Row 3 Knit 1 through back of loop, *knit 2, purl 2; repeat from * until 1 stitch remains, slip that stitch as if to purl with yarn in front.
Repeat until instep is roughly 7" (18 cm) long or 2" (5 cm) from the tip of toe, ending with a wrong side row.

SET UP TOE

Row 1 Knit 1 through back of loop, knit 1, *cross left, cross right, repeat from * until four stitches remain, cross right, knit 1, slip last stitch as if to purl with yarn in front.
Row 2 Knit 1 through back of loop, purl across, slipping last stitch as if to purl with yarn in front.
Place heel stitches on needle and hold 36 instep stitches in reserve. Do not break yarn. Work the heel and sole section using the other end of same ball of yarn or start a second ball of yarn.

HEEL AND SOLE

As the heel and sole are knit, they are joined to the already-knit instep, by picking up stitches along the slipped-stitched instep borders. After the first row, all increases are made immediately before the first marker and after the second marker to form the gussets.

HEEL

Row 1 (RS) Knit 1, place marker, M1R, knit to last stitch, M1L, place marker, slip last stitch as if to knit (with yarn in back), pick up and

knit 1 stitch in the first loop on the side of instep, pass slipped stitch over, turn.

Row 2 Slip first stitch as if to purl with yarn in front and purl across, slipping markers, until 1 stitch remains, slip that stitch as if to purl (with yarn in front), pick up and purl 1 stitch in the next loop on the side of instep, turn.

Row 3 Knit 2 stitches together, M1R, slip marker, *knit 1, slip 1, repeat from * across to marker, slip marker, M1L, slip 1, pick up and knit 1 stitch in the first loop on the side of instep, pass slipped stitch over, turn.

Row 4 Slip first stitch as if to purl with yarn in front and purl across, slipping markers, until 1 stitch remains, slip that stitch as if to purl (with yarn in front), pick up and purl 1 stitch in the first slipped stitch on the side of instep, turn. Repeat rows 3 and 4 until there are a total of 60 stitches (32 heel stitches and 28 gusset stitches), ending with row 4. Remove markers.

TURN THE HEEL

Row 1 Knit 2 stitches together, knit 31, slip slip knit, knit 1, turn.

Row 2 Slip 1, purl 5, purl 2 stitches together, purl 1, turn.

Row 3 Slip 1, knit 6, slip slip knit, knit 1.

Row 4 Slip 1, purl 7, purl 2 stitches together, purl 1.

Continue turning heel, adding 1 stitch in the center section until only 1 unworked stitch remains on each side, ending with a knit row.

Last purl row Slip 1, purl across, slip 2, pick up and purl in the next slipped stitch on the side of the instep, turn.

Last knit row Slip 2 as if to knit, knit 1, and pass both slipped stitches over the knit stitch, knit across to last 2 stitches, slip 2 as if to knit, pick up and knit 1 stitch in the next loop of the instep, pass both slipped stitches over.

SOLE

Continue working the sole back and forth in stockinette stitch and joining the sole to the slipped-stitch edge of the instep until sole and instep are the same length. Try on the sock to ensure that foot length is correct, about 2" (5 cm) from tip of toe. Adjust length, if necessary, by working additional rows of stockinette stitch on instep and then sole.

TOE

Place marker in center of sole stitches to mark beginning of round. Place 36 instep stitches back on needles.

Move 1 stitch from the beginning and 1 stitch from the end of instep stitches to the sole section (34 stitches for sole, 34 stitches for instep).

Round 1 Knit sole stitches until 3 stitches remain, knit 2 stitches together, knit 2, slip slip knit, knit instep stitches until 3 stitches remain, knit 2 stitches together, knit 2, slip slip knit, knit to marker.

Round 2 Knit.

Repeat rounds 1 and 2 until 40 stitches remain.

Repeat round 1 until 20 stitches remain.

FINISHING

Knit across remaining sole stitches. Graft 10 instep stitches to 10 sole stitches. Weave in ends and block.

SHAPED ARCH SOCK

DESIGNED BY KATE WINKLER

KNIT/EXPERIENCED

This clever form-fitting arch shaping was inspired by a pair of similarly shaped stockings by Meg Swansen in *Meg Swansen's Knitting*. It uses Barbara Walker's Baby Cable ribbing on the cuff for decoration, but you could use any small rib or stitch pattern you like with the same stitch multiple. You can knit socks designed specifically for the left or right foot, or two "ambidextrous" socks—there are patterns for all three!

SIZE

Women's M/L

Sample shown 9½" long x 11" around ball of foot (24.1 x 27.9 cm)

MATERIALS

 LION BRAND® LION® CASHMERE BLEND

72% MERINO WOOL, 14% NYLON, 14% CASHMERE

1½ OZ (40 G) 84 YD (71 M) BALL

3 (3) balls #113 Red, or color of your choice

- Set size 5 (3.75 mm) double-pointed needles, *or size to obtain gauge*
- Stitch marker
- Large-eyed, blunt needle

GAUGE

22 stitches + 30 rows = 4" (10 cm) in stockinette stitch.

Be sure to check your gauge.

STITCH EXPLANATION

Baby Cable Ribbing (from Barbara G. Walker's *A Treasury of Knitting Patterns*.)

Rounds 1–3 Knit 2, purl 2 rib.

Round 4 *Knit 2 stitches together, but do not remove from left needle; knit into first stitch again, slip both stitches from left-hand needle, purl 2; repeat from * around.

CUFF

Cast on 52 (56) stitches and distribute over 4 double-pointed needles. Join, being careful not to twist, and place marker to indicate beginning of round.

Work rounds 1–4 of Baby Cable Ribbing pattern 10 times, or to desired length. Work rounds 1–3, decreasing 4 stitches evenly on last round—48 (52) stitches.

Knit 8 rounds.

HEEL FLAP

Knit 12 (13), turn.

Row 1 Slip 1, purl 23 (25).

Row 2 Slip 1, knit 23 (25).

Repeat these 2 rows 8 times, or to desired depth of heel flap.

TURN HEEL

Row 1 Slip 1, purl 13 (15), purl 2 stitches together.

Row 2 Slip 1, knit 6, slip slip knit.

Row 3 Slip 1, purl 6, purl 2 stitches together.

Repeat rows 2 and 3 until all heel stitches have been worked, ending with Row 2—8 heel stitches.

GUSSET

Pick up and knit stitches along one side of heel flap, M1 by lifting yarn between last stitch on heel flap and instep stitches, knit across next 2 needles (instep), M1 by lifting yarn between last stitch on heel flap and instep stitches, pick up and knit stitches on other side of heel flap, knit 4 heel stitches onto same needle—52 (54) stitches.

Beginning at center of sole, knit to 3 stitches from end of needle 1, slip slip knit, knit 1; work across next 2 needles; knit 1, knit 2 stitches together, knit to end of needle 4—50 (52) stitches. Work 4 rounds even.

ARCH SHAPING

RIGHT SOCK

Round 1 Beginning at center of sole, knit 1, M1, knit 2, slip slip knit, knit to end of needle 1; knit across next 2 needles; knit to 5 stitches from end of needle 4, knit 2 stitches together, knit 2, M1, knit 1.

Round 2 and all even-numbered rounds Knit.

Round 3 Knit 1, M1, knit 3, slip slip knit, knit to 6 stitches from end of needle 4, knit 2 stitches together, knit 3, M1, knit 1.

Round 5 Knit 1, M1, knit 4, slip slip knit, knit to 7 stitches from end of needle 4, knit 2 stitches together, knit 4, M1, knit 1.

Round 7 Knit 1, M1, knit 4, slip slip knit, knit to 8 stitches from end of needle 4, knit 2 stitches together, knit 5, M1, knit 1.

Round 9 Knit 1, M1, knit 4, slip slip knit, knit to 9 stitches from end of needle 4, knit 2 stitches together, knit 6, M1, knit 1.

Round 11 Knit 1, M1, knit 4, slip slip knit, knit to 10 stitches from end of needle 4, knit 2 stitches together, knit 7, M1, knit 1.

Round 13 Knit 1, M1, knit 4, slip slip knit, knit to 11 stitches from end of needle 4, knit 2 stitches together, knit 8, M1, knit 1.

Continue arch shaping until sock is 2" (5 cm) shorter than desired finished length. Note that at some point you will have to work the decrease with stitches from needles 3 **and** 4, then on the third needle thereafter. The decrease line will wrap around the top of your foot.

LEFT SOCK

Round 1 Beginning at center of heel, knit 1, M1, knit 2, slip slip knit, knit to end of first needle; knit across next 2 needles; knit to 5 stitches from end of needle 4, knit 2 stitches together, knit 2, M1, knit 1.

Round 2 and all even-numbered rounds Knit.

Round 3 Knit 1, M1, knit 3, slip slip knit, knit to 6 stitches from end of needle 4, knit 2 stitches together, knit 3, M1, knit 1.

Round 5 Knit 1, M1, knit 4, slip slip knit, knit to 7 stitches from end of needle 4, knit 2 stitches together, knit 4, M1, knit 1.

Round 7 Knit 1, M1, knit 5, slip slip knit, knit to 7 stitches from end of needle 4, knit 2 stitches together, knit 4, M1, knit 1.

Round 9 Knit 1, M1, knit 6, slip slip knit, knit to 7 stitches from end of needle 4, knit 2 stitches together, knit 4, M1, knit 1.

Round 11 Knit 1, M1, knit 7, slip slip knit, knit to 7 stitches from end of needle 4, knit 2 stitches together, knit 4, M1, knit 1.

Round 13 Knit 1, M1, knit 8, slip slip knit, knit to 7 stitches from end of needle 4, knit 2 stitches together, knit 4, M1, knit 1.

Continue arch shaping until sock is 2" (5 cm) shorter than desired finished length.

AMBIDEXTROUS ARCH SHAPING
For an alternative to equalize wear, work symmetrical arch shaping centered on the sole as follows.

Round 1 Beginning at center of heel, knit 1, M1, knit 2, slip slip knit, knit to end of needle 1; knit across next 2 needles; knit to 5 stitches from end of needle 4, knit 2 stitches together, knit 2, M1, knit 1.

Round 2 and all even-numbered rounds Knit.

Round 3 Knit 1, M1, knit 3, slip slip knit, knit to 6 stitches from end of needle 4, knit 2 stitches together, knit 3, M1, knit 1.

Round 5 Knit 1, M1, knit 4, slip slip knit, knit to 7 stitches from end of needle 4, knit 2 stitches together, knit 4, M1, knit 1.

Round 7 Knit 1, M1, knit 5, slip slip knit, knit to 8 stitches from end of needle 4, knit 2 stitches together, knit 5, M1, knit 1.

Round 9 Knit 1, M1, knit 6, slip slip knit, knit to 9 stitches from end of needle 4, knit 2 stitches together, knit 6, M1, knit 1.

Round 11 Knit 1, M1, knit 7, slip slip knit, knit to 10 stitches from end of needle 4, knit 2 stitches

together, knit 7, M1, knit 1.

Round 13 Knit 1, M1, knit 8, slip slip knit, knit to 11 stitches from end of needle 4, knit 2 stitches together, knit 8, M1, knit 1. Continue arch shaping until slip slip knit and knit 2 stitches together meet on top of foot. Knit to 2" (5 cm) from desired sock length.

SHAPE TOE
Beginning at center of heel, knit to 3 stitches from end of needle 1, slip slip knit, knit 1; knit 1, knit 2 stitches together, work to end of needle 2; knit to 3 stitches from end of needle 3, slip slip knit, knit 1; knit 1, knit 2 stitches together, work to end of needle 4. Knit 1 round even.

Decrease every other round as described above until 20 (24) stitches remain or desired length is reached. Break yarn, leaving a 12" (30.5 cm) tail. Graft remaining stitches. Weave in ends and block.

BLUEBIRD LACE SOCK

DESIGNED BY ANDI SMITH FOR KNITBRIT
CROCHET/INTERMEDIATE

Durable yet feminine, these soft socks can be machine-washed.
They look exceptionally cute with sandals or clogs.

SIZE
Women's M/L
Sample shown 10" long x 11"
around ball of foot (25.4 x 27.9 cm)

MATERIALS
 LION BRAND® BABYSOFT®
60% ACRYLIC, 40% POLYAMID
5 OZ (141 G) 459 YD (420 M) BALL

1 ball #102 Aqua, or color of
your choice

- Size F-5 (3.75 mm) crochet hook,
  or size to obtain gauge
- Large-eyed, blunt needle

GAUGE
16 single crochet and 20 rows = 4"
(10 cm).
Be sure to check your gauge.

PATTERN NOTES
This sock starts at the toe and is
worked in the round.

STITCH EXPLANATIONS
fpdc (Front Post Double Crochet)
Yarn over, put hook around the
front of the post made by double
crochet on previous round, yarn
over, pull hook through, and work
double crochet.
bpdc (Back Post Double Crochet)
Yarn over, put hook around the
back of the post made by double
crochet on previous round, yarn
over, pull hook through, and work
double crochet.

TOE
Chain 12.
Round 1 2 single crochet into 2nd
chain from hook, single crochet
into top loop of next 9 chains, 2
single crochet into last chain and

rotate work so that the bottom
loops of the chain are now at the
top, single crochet into each loop.
Round 2 Single crochet, 2 single
crochet into next loop, work to
2 single crochet before rotate, 2
single crochet into next loop, single
crochet, rotate, and repeat.
Continue to increase by 4 single
crochet each round until you have
48 single crochets.
Next 2 rounds Single crochet
without increase.

FOOT
Working in the round, half double
crochet into next loop, chain 1,
skip loop, half double crochet into
next loop. Continue working half
double crochet, chain 1, skip 1, half
double crochet. (As you get to the
second round, the half double
crochets will go into the chain 1
space of the previous round).

Continue working in the round until piece measures 7" (18 cm) or desired length. End at side of foot so that the toes lay flat.

HEEL
Row 1 Single crochet 24 across base of foot, turn.
Row 2 Single crochet 23 across (last single crochet of previous row is unworked), turn.
Row 3 Single crochet 22 across, turn.
Continue in this manner until 10 single crochet remain.

HEEL TURN
Row 1 Single crochet across remaining 10 single crochet (do not turn), single crochet twice down the side, once into the previous row, and once into the next unworked stitch, turn—12 single crochet.
Row 2 Skip first single crochet, single crochet into 11, single crochet twice down side as in previous row, turn—13 single crochet.
Repeat row 2 until you reach the bottom of the heel—28 single crochet.

HEEL GUSSET
Resume working half double crochet, chain 1, pattern working half double crochets into 2 chain-1 spaces at either side of the instep on next and following row.

LEG
Continue in pattern for about 3" (7.5 cm) or desired length.

CUFF
Round 1 Double crochet into each space—48 double crochet.
Round 2 Chain 2, (fpdc, bpdc) to end of round, joining with a slip stitch.
Round 3 Work as for round 2.
Work 2 more rounds, fasten off, and weave in ends.

WHITBY LACE SOCK

DESIGNED BY ANDI SMITH FOR KNITBRIT

CROCHET/INTERMEDIATE

Another crocheted lace wonder, these socks will dress up any outfit . . . even if you're just watching TV on the couch!

SIZE

Women's L
Sample shown 9½" long x 11" around ball of foot (24.1 x 27.9 cm)

MATERIALS

 LION BRAND® LION® WOOL
100% WOOL
3 OZ (85 G) 158 YD (144 M) BALL

2 balls #132 Lemongrass, or color of your choice

- Size F-5 (3.75 mm) crochet hook, *or size to obtain gauge*
- Large-eyed, blunt needle

GAUGE

12 sts and 15 rows = 4" (10 cm). *Be sure to check your gauge.*

LEG

Loosely chain 36 stitches; join with a slip stitch.

Round 1 Chain 5, skip 3, single crochet into next loop, repeat to 3 chains before end of round, chain 3, double crochet into first chain of round—9 chain 5 loops.
Round 2 3 double crochet cluster into single crochet, single crochet into 5 chain space, repeat to end.
Round 3 Slip stitch into next 2 loops in 3 double crochet cluster, chain 5, chain into center loop of next 3 double crochet cluster, repeat to last pattern, chain 3, double crochet into center loop of first 3 double crochet cluster.
Rounds 2 and 3 form pattern. Repeat until desired length of leg, ending with round 2.

HEEL

Row 1 Slip 2 into next 3 double crochet cluster as if you were going to start round 3, turn, chain 1, single crochet across bottom of sock, turn—18 double clusters.
Row 2 Chain 1, single crochet 17, turn.
Row 3 Chain 1, single crochet 16, turn.
Continue until 8 single crochet remain.

HEEL TURN

Row 1 Single crochet across remaining 8 single crochet (do not turn), single crochet twice down the side, once into the previous row and once into the next unworked stitch, turn—10 single crochet.
Row 2 Skip first single crochet, single crochet into 9, single crochet twice down side as in previous row, turn—11 single crochet.
Repeat row 2 until you reach the bottom of the heel, turn—20 single crochet.
Next row Single crochet, single

crochet 2 together, single crochet to last 3 single crochet, single crochet 2 together, single crochet—18 single crochet.

FOOT

Continue in established pattern, keeping continuity from leg, and work until the foot measures around 7" (18 cm) (or to base of toes), finishing with round 2 of pattern.

TOE SHAPING

Round 1 Chain 1, single crochet 36 evenly around; do not join, keep working in the round.

Round 2 Single crochet, single crochet 2 together, single crochet 12, single crochet 2 together, single crochet 2, single crochet 2 together, single crochet 12, single crochet 2 together, single crochet—32 single crochet.

Round 3 Single crochet.

Round 4 Single crochet, single crochet 2 together, single crochet 10, single crochet 2 together, single crochet 2, single crochet 2 together, single crochet 10, single crochet 2 together, single crochet—28 single crochet.

Round 5 Single crochet.

Round 6 Single crochet, single crochet 2 together, single crochet 8, single crochet 2 together, single crochet 2, single crochet 2 together, single crochet 8, single crochet 2 together, single crochet—24 single crochet.

Round 7 Single crochet.

Finish off by sewing toe seam together and weaving in any loose ends.

CHEVRON LACE SOCKS

DESIGNED BY SUSAN PIERCE LAWRENCE
KNIT/EXPERIENCED

Sophisticated lace and shaping combined with a pow! blast of color makes these socks one of a kind.

SIZE

Women's M
Sample shown 9½" long x 10" around ball of foot (24.1 x 25.4 cm)

MATERIALS

 LION BRAND® BABYSOFT®
60% ACRYLIC, 40% POLYAMIDE
5 OZ (141 G) 459 YD (420 M) BALL

1 ball #103 Bubblegum, or color of your choice
- Set of size 4 (3.5 mm) double-pointed needles, *or size to obtain gauge*
- Stitch marker
- Stitch holders or smooth waste yarn
- Large-eyed, blunt needle

GAUGE

24 stitches + 32 rows = 4" (10 cm) in stockinette stitch.
Be sure to check your gauge.

STITCH EXPLANATIONS

Leg Stitch Pattern
Round 1 *Knit 1, knit 2 stitches together, knit 3, yarn over, knit 1, yarn over, knit 3, slip slip knit; repeat from * 4 times.
Rounds 2 and 4 Knit.
Round 3 *Knit 1, knit 2 stitches together, knit 2, yarn over, knit 3, yarn over, knit 2, slip slip knit; repeat from * 4 times.

Instep Stitch Pattern
Round 1 *Knit 1, knit 2 stitches together, knit 3, yarn over, knit 1, yarn over, knit 3, slip slip knit; repeat from * 2 times, knit 1.
Rounds 2 and 4 Knit.
Round 3 *Knit 1, knit 2 stitches together, knit 2, yarn over, knit 3, yarn over, knit 2, slip slip knit; repeat from * 2 times, knit 1.

CUFF

Loosely cast on 48 stitches. Divide evenly onto 4 double-pointed needles (12 stitches on each needle) and join into the round, being careful not to twist. Place marker at the beginning of the round.
Rounds 1, 3, and 5 Purl.
Rounds 2, 4, and 6 Knit.

LEG

Repeat Leg Stitch Pattern until the leg of the sock is approximately 6–7" (15–18 cm) long, measured from the cast-on edge. End by working round 4 of the stitch pattern.
Place the next 25 stitches onto a piece of waste yarn or stitch holder

to reserve for the instep. Place the remaining 23 stitches onto one needle for the heel flap. Turn work so the wrong side is facing.

HEEL FLAP

Row 1 (WS) Slip 1, knit 2, purl 17, knit 2, purl 1, turn.

Row 2 Slip 1, knit 22, turn.

Repeat last 2 rows 10 times then repeat row 1 once more; you have now worked a total of 21 heel flap rows. The heel flap should be slightly more than 2" (5 cm) long.

TURN HEEL

Row 1 Slip 1, knit 14, slip slip knit, turn.

Row 2 Slip 1, purl 7, purl 2 stitches together, turn.

Row 3: Slip 1, knit 7, slip slip knit, turn.

Repeat Rows 2 and 3 until you've worked all the heel stitches, ending by working row 2.

With right side facing, knit across remaining 9 heel stitches.

GUSSETS

Place 5 heel stitches onto one needle (needle 1); place the 25 instep stitches onto a second needle (needle 2); place the remaining 4 heel stitches onto a third needle (needle 3).

Using needle 1, pick up and knit 12 stitches along the side of the heel flap.

Work the stitches on needle 2 according to the Instep Stitch Pattern, beginning with round 1. Pick up and knit 12 stitches along the other side of the heel flap and knit the 4 stitches from needle 3. Begin the gusset decreases as follows:

Round 1 Needle 1: Knit to last 3 stitches, k2tog, knit 1. Needle 2: Work stitches in established Instep Stitch Pattern. Needle 3: Knit 1, slip slip knit, knit to end.

Round 2 Needle 1: Knit to end. Needle 2: Work stitches in established Instep Stitch Pattern. Needle 3: Knit to end.

Repeat these 2 rounds until you have decreased back down to 48 stitches.

FOOT

Work even in the established pattern on the instep and stockinette on the sole until the foot of the sock measures approximately 2" (5 cm) less than the total desired length.

TOE

Round 1 Knit to end of round.

Round 2 *Knit 4, knit 2 stitches together; repeat from * to end of round—42 stitches.

Rounds 3–6 Knit.

Round 7 *Knit 3, knit 2 stitches together; repeat from * to end of round—36 stitches.

Rounds 8–10 Knit.

Round 11 *Knit 2, knit 2 stitches together; repeat from * to end of round—24 stitches.

Rounds 12–13 Knit.

Round 14 *Knit 1, knit 2 stitches together; repeat from * to end of round—16 stitches.

Round 15 Knit.

Round 16 *Knit 2 stitches together; repeat from * to end of round—8 stitches.

Break yarn, leaving a long tail. Thread through 8 remaining stitches and pull snug to close the opening. Weave in ends and block.

3.
COLORWORK

Color makes the world go 'round, if these socks are any indication. Clever juxtapositions of multicolor yarns with their solid counterparts, Fair Isle patterns, and much more await you in this chapter.

AUTUMN ROADSIDE SOCK

DESIGNED BY LINDA DIAK

CROCHET/BEGINNER

These colorful socks will remind you of leaves on the side of the road in early fall.

SIZE
Women's M/L
Sample shown 10½" long x 10" around ball of foot (26.7 x 25.4 cm)

MATERIALS

 LION BRAND® LION® WOOL
100% WOOL
3 OZ (85 G) 158 YD (144 M) BALL

1 ball each #099 Winter White (A), #132 Lemongrass (B), #187 Goldenrod (C), #133 Pumpkin (D), #153 Ebony (E), or colors of your choice

- Size G-4 (4 mm) hook, *or size to obtain gauge*
- Stitch markers
- Large-eyed, blunt needle

GAUGE
16 single crochet and 16 rows = 4" (10 cm).
Be sure to check your gauge.

NOTES
When joining new colors, work single crochet until there are 2 loops on the hook. Drop or carry old color behind work and pull new color through both loops on hook. Stitch over loose ends to avoid having to weave them in later. Two yarns can be tensioned at once by using the middle finger of the yarn-holding hand for one color and the thumb for the other color. If this is uncomfortable or awkward at first, it can be helpful to give a little tug on the stitches after color changes to maintain even stitching.

TOE
With E, chain 5.

Round 1 Worked in one continuous spiral without joining, single crochet in 2nd chain from hook and in each of next 3 chain, chain 1, turn.
Single crochet in opposite side of next 4 chain, chain 1, turn.
Single crochet in each of next 4 single crochet, 3 single crochet in next chain 1, single crochet in each of next 4 single crochet, 3 single crochet in next chain 1, single crochet in each of next 5 single crochet, 3 single crochet in next single crochet, single crochet in each of next 5 single crochet, 3 single crochet in next single crochet, single crochet in each of next 8 single crochet, 3 single crochet in next single crochet, single crochet in each of next 8 single crochet, 3 single crochet in next single crochet, single crochet in each of next 9 single crochet, 3 single crochet in next single crochet, single crochet in each of next 10 single crochet, 3 single crochet in next single crochet, single crochet in each of next 10 single crochet, 3 single crochet in next single crochet.

From this point on the sock will continue to be worked in the round; however, a chain 1 or chain 2 will be worked at the start of each round and a slip stitch will be worked into this chain at the end of the round. Working this way will prevent the stitch pattern from slanting and enable the color changes to match at the seam.

Round 2 Chain 1, single crochet in next single crochet, place marker to mark the first stitch of the round, single crochet in each single crochet around. Join with slip stitch into chain 1—26 single crochet.

Round 3 Chain 1, single crochet in each single crochet around. Change to B. Join with slip stitch in beginning chain 1.

Round 4 Chain 1, continue working in single crochet, alternating colors B and E around. Join with slip stitch in beginning chain 1.

Rounds 5–7 Chain 1, single crochet in each single crochet around, working 1 row each in B, C, and D. Join with slip stitch in beginning chain 1.

Round 8 Repeat round 4, alternating colors D and B around.

Round 9 Repeat round 4, alternating colors B and D around.

Round 10 With B, chain 1, single crochet in each single crochet. Join with slip stitch in beginning chain 1.

Round 11 With C, repeat Round 10. Change to A.

BODY

Round 1 With A, chain 2, skip first single crochet, *(2 single crochet, chain 2, 2 single crochet) all in next single crochet, skip next 2 single crochet; repeat from * 7 more times, ending (2 single crochet, chain 2, 2 single crochet) all in last single crochet. Join with slip stitch into beginning chain 2-space—9 chain 2-spaces.

Rounds 2–5 Chain 2, (2 single crochet, chain 2, 2 single crochet) all into each chain 2-space around. Join with slip stitch into beginning chain 2-space.

Note: If you wish to lengthen the body of the sock, repeat round 2 to desired length.

Round 6 Repeat round 2. Change to B.

Round 7 Repeat round 2. Change to D.

Round 8 Chain 2, beginning in first chain 2-space *single crochet in chain 2-space, skip next single crochet, half double crochet in each

of next two single crochet, skip next single crochet; repeat from * 7 more times, single crochet in next chain 2-space, skip next single crochet, half double crochet in each of next 2 single crochet. Change to D.

Join with slip stitch in beginning chain 2-space.

Create a space for the heel:

Chain 1, single crochet in each of next 13 single crochet, chain 15, single crochet in each of last 2 single crochet. Join with slip stitch in beginning chain 1—30 stitches.

ANKLE/CUFF

Round 1 Chain 2, skip next single crochet, *(2 single crochet, chain 2, 2 single crochet) all in next single crochet, skip next 2 single crochet; repeat from * 4 more times, (2 single crochet, chain 2, 2 single crochet) in first chain, skip next 2 chain, **(2 single crochet, chain 2, 2 single crochet) all in next chain, skip next 2 chain; repeat from ** 4 more times, (2 single crochet, chain 2, 2 single crochet) in next chain. Change to C. Skip last single crochet. Join with slip stitch in beginning chain 2-space—10 chain 2-spaces.

Round 2 Chain 2, *(2 single crochet, chain 2, 2 single crochet) in next chain 2-space; repeat from * 9 more times. Change to A. Join with slip stitch in beginning chain 2-space.

Rounds 3–4 Repeat round 2. Note: For a longer cuff, repeat round 3 until desired length is achieved.

Round 5 (or last round before Cuff Edge) Repeat round 2. Change to C.

CUFF EDGE

Chain 2, *single crochet in chain 2-space, skip next single crochet, half double crochet in each of next 2 single crochet, skip next single crochet; repeat from * 8 more times, single crochet in next chain 2-space, skip next single crochet, half double crochet in each of next 2 single crochet. Join with slip stitch in beginning chain 2-space. Fasten off. Using large-eyed, blunt needle, weave in ends.

HEEL

Join E at corner of heel space. Single crochet in each of next 15 single crochet (bottom of heel), work 15 single crochet evenly around top edge of heel. Join with slip stitch in first single crochet—30 single crochet.

The heel is worked in a spiral round without joining. To keep track of rounds, place a marker in the first stitch of each round. Move the marker as you work each new round.

Round 1 Chain 1, single crochet in each of next 12 single crochet, (single crochet 2 together over next 2 single crochet) twice, single crochet in each of next 12 single crochet, single crochet 2 together over next 2 single crochet. Do not join to beginning of round—27 single crochet.

Round 2 Single crochet 2 together over next 2 single crochet, single crochet in each of next 9 single crochet, (single crochet 2 together over next 2 single crochet) twice, single crochet in each of next 10 single crochet, single crochet 2 together over next 2 single crochet—23 single crochet.

Round 3 Single crochet 2 together over next 2 single crochet, single crochet in each of next 7 single crochet, (single crochet 2 together over next 2 single crochet) twice, single crochet in each of next 8 single crochet, single crochet 2 together over next 2 single crochet—19 single crochet.

Round 4 Single crochet 2 together over next 2 single crochet, single crochet in each of next 5 single crochet, (single crochet 2 together over next 2 single crochet) twice, single crochet in each of next 6 single crochet, single crochet 2 together over next 2 single crochet—15 single crochet.

Round 5 Single crochet 2 together over next 2 single crochet, single crochet in each of next 3 single crochet, (single crochet 2 together over next 2 single crochet) twice, single crochet in each of next 4 single crochet, single crochet 2 together over next 2 single crochet—11 single crochet.

Round 6 Single crochet 2 together over next 2 single crochet, single crochet in each of next 2 single crochet, single crochet 2 together over next 2 single crochet, single crochet in each of next 3 single crochet, single crochet 2 together over next 2 single crochet—8 single crochet.

Lengthen the loop on the hook, turn heel inside out, and pull loop and a length of the working yarn through the hole. Work 5 slip stitch around to close.

Fasten off. Using large-eyed, blunt needle, weave in ends.

NORWEGIAN-STYLE FOOTED SLIPPERS

KNIT/INTERMEDIATE

These beautiful slippers, styled in the manner of traditional Norwegian slippers, are a joy to knit. The colors shown here are common in Norwegian knitting, but for extra sass, you could change to brighter tones.

SIZE

Women's M/L
Sample shown 9½" long x 11" around ball of foot (24.1 x 27.9 cm)

MATERIALS

 LION BRAND® LION® WOOL
100% WOOL
3 OZ (85 G) 158 YD (144 M) BALL

2 balls each #099 Winter White (A), #153 Ebony (B), and #113 Scarlet (C), or colors of your choice
• Set of 5 size 5 (3.75 mm) double-pointed needles, *or size to obtain gauge*
• Set of 5 size 3 (3.25 mm) double-pointed needles, *or size to obtain gauge*
• Large-eyed, blunt needle

• Optional: leather slipper soles (available at craft and yarn shops)

GAUGE

24 stitches + 25 rounds = 4" (10 cm) measured in stranded pattern. *Be sure to check your gauge.*

CUFF

Using A and smaller needles, cast on 56 stitches. Divide stitches evenly onto 4 needles and join in the round, being careful not to twist.
Work in knit 1, purl 1 ribbing for 3 rounds.
Knit 2 rounds.
Change to larger needles and work Chart A.
Knit 1 round with A.

HEEL FLAP

Work heel flap back and forth over 27 stitches in Chart B (reserve the remaining instep stitches on an extra needle or stitch holder) for 16 rows. Adjust stitches so that there are 13 on the first needle and 13 on the second. Fold the heel flap in half, with right sides on the inside.
Work 3-needle bind-off to join edges. Cut yarn.

GUSSET

Hold sock with the cuff opening on the right and the heel on the left. With the left-side instep needle, pick up one stitch between the instep and the heel flap. Working in Chart B and with a new needle, pick up 16 stitches along the left side of the heel flap; 2 stitches from the seam at the center/bottom of the heel flap; 16 stitches along the right side of the heel flap. (35 stitches picked up, 64 stitches total.) Work across instep in Chart C. Decrease at beginning and ending of sole (Chart B) stitches every other round 4 times—56 stitches remaining.

FOOT

Continue working sole in Chart B and instep in Chart C until about 2 inches (5 cm) less than desired length.

TOE

The toe is color-patterned in vertical stripes: 1 stitch A, 1 stitch B.
Round 1 Needles 1 and 3: Knit 2 stitches together, work to end of needle. Needles 2 and 4: Work to last 2 stitches, slip slip knit.

Round 2 Knit in color pattern as established.
Work these 2 rounds 4 times, then work round 1 (decrease round) every round until 6 stitches remain on each needle. Graft toe with Kitchener stitch. Weave in ends and block.

FINISHING

Stitch slipper soles on to the bottom following the package's directions if desired.

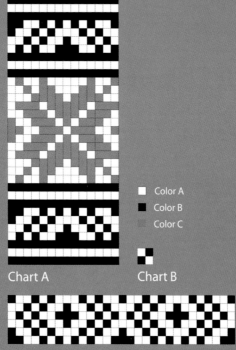

Color A
Color B
Color C

Chart A   Chart B

Chart C

BIRD'S EYE CHILDREN'S SLIPPERS

DESIGNED BY TERRI SHEA

KNIT/INTERMEDIATE

These slippers are styled after traditional Norwegian stockings. Each section of the sock features a different pattern, which simplifies the construction once you've figured out how the patterns go together. Knitters in Selbu, Norway, created fantastic designs in blue and white that came to represent Norwegian knitting. They are still popular today. Knit these slippers for après-ski or anytime.

SIZE

Average child's foot

Sample shown 9" long x 11" around ball of foot (22.9 x 27.9 cm)

MATERIALS

 LION BRAND® LION® WOOL
100% WOOL

3 OZ (85 G) 158 YD (144 M) BALL

1 ball #099 Winter White (A),
2 balls #111 Midnight Blue (B),
or colors of your choice

- Set of 5 size 5 (3.75 mm) double-pointed needles, *or size to obtain gauge*
- Set of 5 size 3 (3.25 mm) double-pointed needles, *or size to obtain gauge*
- Smooth waste yarn
- Large-eyed, blunt needle

GAUGE

24 stitches and 25 rounds = 4" (10 cm) measured over cuff pattern. *Be sure to check your gauge.*

CUFF

Using A and smaller needles, cast on 48 stitches. Divide stitches evenly onto 4 needles and join in the round, being careful not to twist. Work in knit 1, purl 1 ribbing for 3 rounds. Knit 2 rounds. Change to larger needles and work

Chart A. Knit 1 round in A.

HEEL FLAP

Slip last stitch from previous round to the working needle. Work heel flap back and forth over slipped stitch plus the next 25 stitches in Chart B for 16 rows (26 stitches in heel flap). Divide stitches evenly onto two needles and fold the heel flap in half, with right sides on the inside. Work 3-needle bind-off to join ends. Cut yarn.

GUSSET

Hold sock with the cuff opening on the right and the heel on the left. With the left-side instep needle,

pick up 1 stitch between the instep and the heel flap. Working in Chart B and a new needle, pick up 16 stitches along the left side of the heel flap, 2 stitches from the seam at the center/bottom of the heel flap, 16 stitches along the right side of the heel flap, and 1 stitch between the heel flap and the instep stitches—36 stitches picked up, 58 stitches total. Move the last stitch picked up between the heel flap and instep to the instep needles, and work across instep in Chart C. Decrease at beginning and ending of sole (Chart B) stitches every other round 5 times— 48 stitches.

FOOT

Continue working sole in Chart B and instep in Chart C as shown, to about 2" (5 cm) less than desired foot measurement.

TOE

The toe is color-patterned in vertical stripes: one stitch A, one stitch B.

Round 1 Needles 1 and 3: Knit 2 stitches together, work to end of needle. Needles 2 and 4: Work to last 2 stitches, slip slip knit.

Round 2 Knit in color pattern as established.

Work these 2 rounds 4 times, then work round 1 (decrease round) every round until 8 stitches remain on each needle. Graft remaining stitches with Kitchener stitch. Weave in ends and block.

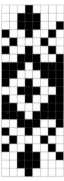

Chart A

Chart B

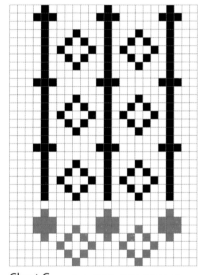

Chart C   Grey motifs are for placement only—do not knit them on instep.

☐ Color A   ■ Color B

SQUARES & STRIPES SOCKS

DESIGNED BY CHRISSY GARDINER

KNIT/EASY

These colorful socks can be knit in many combinations for a different look each time. Try out your favorite tones!

SIZE

Women's M

Sample shown 8" long x 8" around ball of foot (20 x 20 cm)

MATERIALS

 LION BRAND® MICROSPUN
100% MICROFIBER ACRYLIC
2½ OZ (70 G) 168 YD (154 M) BALL

2 balls #109 Royal Blue (A) and 1 skein #186 Mango (B), or colors of your choice
• Set of 5 size 2 (2.75 mm) double-pointed needles, *or size to obtain gauge*
• Large-eyed, blunt needle

GAUGE

6.5 stitches + 8 rows = 1" (2.5 cm) in stockinette stitch.
6.5 stitches + 9 rows = 1" (2.5 cm) in squares & stripes pattern.
Be sure to check your gauge.

SQUARES & STRIPES PATTERN

(Over 2 stitches and 8 rounds)

Rounds 1 and 2 With B, *knit 1, slip 1, repeat from * to end of round.
Round 3 With A, knit to end of round.
Round 4 With A, purl to end of round.
Round 5 With B, knit to end of round.
Round 6 With B, purl to end of round.
Round 7 With A, knit to end of round.
Round 8 With A, purl to end of round.

CUFF

With A, cast on 50 stitches and divide them over 4 double-pointed needles as follows: Needle 1: 13 stitches. Needle 2: 13 stitches. Needle 3: 12 stitches. Needle 4: 12 stitches.

Join stitches without twisting and begin working in the round.
Needles 1 and 4 will hold the heel stitches, needles 2 and 3 the instep stitches.
Work in knit 1, purl 1 rib for 8 rounds.
Next round, begin working Squares & Stripes Pattern across all needles.
End with round 8 of pattern when cuff measures approximately 8" (20 cm) from top or desired length.
The rest of the foot of the sock will be worked only with A.

HEEL FLAP

Knit all of needle 1's stitches onto needle 4, knitting the first 2 stitches on needle 1 together.
You will now start working the heel flap back and forth on 24 stitches.
Row 1 (WS) Slip 1, purl to end.
Row 2 *Slip 1, knit 1; repeat from * to end.

Repeat rows 1 and 2, 16 times (there should be 16 selvedge stitches along edge of heel flap). Work row 1 once more.

TURN HEEL

Row 1 (RS) Knit 15, slip slip knit, turn.

Row 2 Slip 1, purl 6, purl 2 stitches together, turn.

Row 3 Slip 1, knit 6, slip slip knit, turn.

Repeat rows 2 and 3 until 8 heel stitches remain, ending with row 2.

HEEL GUSSET

Knit across the 8 heel stitches. Working up the side of the heel flap, pick up and knit 16 stitches (this is now needle 1).

Work instep section on needles 2 and 3 in stockinette stitch, knitting the last 2 stitches of needle 2 together. There should now be 12 stitches on each of needles 2 and 3.

Using empty needle (needle 4), pick up and knit 16 stitches down other side of heel flap, then knit the first 4 stitches on needle 1 onto needle 4.

To shape the heel gusset, work the following rounds:

Round 1 Needle 1: Work to last 3 stitches, knit 2 stitches together, knit 1. Needles 2 and 3: Work even. Needle 4: Knit 1, slip slip knit, work to end of needle.

Round 2 Work even across all needles.

Repeat rows 1 and 2 until you have 12 stitches remaining on each of needles 1 and 4—48 stitches total across all needles.

FOOT

Continue working in stockinette stitch across all needles.

Work until foot measures 7" (18 cm) or 2" (5 cm) less than desired finished length, ending with needle 3.

TOE

Round 1 Needle 4: Knit 1, slip slip knit, work to end of needle. Needle 1: Work to last 3 stitches, knit 2 stitches together, knit 1. Needle 2: Knit 1, slip slip knit, work to end of needle. Needle 3: Work to last 3 stitches, knit 2 stitches together, knit 1.

Round 2 Knit all stitches.

Repeat rounds 1 and 2, 6 times (until there are 6 stitches left on each needle).

Repeat round 1, 4 times (until there are 2 stitches left on each needle).

Cut yarn, leaving an 8" (20 cm) tail. Using a large-eyed, blunt needle, thread yarn tail through remaining toe stitches and pull tight.

FINISHING

Weave in ends. Lay socks flat to block or use sock blockers.

OP ART SOCKS

DESIGNED BY LAURA ANDERSSON FOR SIRIUS KNITTING
KNIT/EXPERIENCED

This sock is both modern and mod—it's reminiscent of 1960s patterning, with a twist.

SIZE

Women's S (M, L)
Sample shown 8¾ (9¼, 9¾)"
(22 [23.5, 25] cm)

MATERIALS

 LION BRAND® BABYSOFT®
60% ACRYLIC, 40% POLYAMID
4 OZ (113 G) 459 YD (420 M) BALL

1 ball each #153 Black (A) and #100 White (B), or colors of your choice
- Size 3 (3.25 mm) double-pointed needles, *or size to obtain gauge*
- Size 2 (2.75 mm) double-pointed needles, *or size to obtain gauge*
- Large-eyed, blunt needle
- Stitch markers

GAUGE

34 stitches per 4" (10 cm) in stockinette on larger needles.
38 stitches per 4" (10 cm) over stranded pattern on foot.
Be sure to check your gauge.

NOTES

The stranded pattern will make your knitting tighter than it would be in plain stockinette; be sure to swatch first and use the needle sizes necessary to match the specified gauge.

RUFFLE

Throughout ruffle, always alternate between colors, that is, knit 1 A, 1 B, 1 A, 1 B, etc. After decreasing your colors will jog to create a pattern.

Using size 3 needles, cast on 216 stitches using two-color long-tail cast-on. (The first stitch is the slip knot of the first color, the second stitch is the slip knot of the second color; from there, continue to cast on normally, alternating colors, bringing both tails of yarn in the working color under the last stitch of the opposite color before creating the next stitch.) Turn work. Purl 1 row, then join, being careful not to twist, and place marker. Knit 1 round.

Decrease Round *Knit 1, knit 2 stitches together, repeat from * around—144 stitches.

Plain Round Knit.

Repeat these 2 rounds once more—96 stitches.

Follow the directions below for the size of sock you are knitting, then continue at "All Sizes."

LARGE

Decrease Round *Knit 2, knit 2 stitches together; repeat from * around—72 stitches.

MEDIUM

Decrease Round *Knit 1, knit 2 stitches together; repeat from * around—64 stitches.

SMALL

Decrease Round *Knit 1, knit 2 stitches together; repeat from * around—64 stitches.

Plain Round Knit.

Decrease Round: *Knit 2, knit 2 stitches together, repeat from * around—48 stitches.

ALL SIZES

Continue here with 3-row Swedish Braid.

Round 1 Knit across, alternating colors.

Round 2 Bring both yarns to the front and purl around, alternating A and B stitches. Be careful to start so that your first stitch is not the same color as the first stitch in the round below.

Round 3 Return both strands to the back and knit around alternating the 2 yarns; be sure that each stitch is opposite that in the round below.

TURN THE RUFFLE

To make the ruffle turn down, switch the direction of knitting as follows: Make 1 stitch by lifting the bar between the stitch on the right needle and the next stitch on the left needle, and place this stitch on the right needle. Turn the work inside out and prepare to knit back the other way. Knit the newly made stitch together with the first stitch and continue to knit following the patterns below—48 (64, 72) stitches.

LEG DESIGNS

Both colors are carried throughout. When using only 1 color in a round, twist the second (non-working color) with the working color at the start of the round. In this way, the nonworking yarn is carried to the next round.

Knit 14 rounds in Fibonacci Stripes Pattern as follows:

Round 1 B.
Round 2 A.
Round 3 B.
Round 4 A.
Rounds 5–6 B.
Rounds 7–8 A.
Rounds 9–11 B.
Rounds 12–14 A.

Work 7 rounds in Piano Keys Pattern as follows:

Round 1 Knit with A.

Rounds 2–6 Work 5 rounds of *knit 2 A, knit 2 B; repeat from * around.

Round 7 Knit with B.

Work 8 rounds in Crescent Pattern as follows:

Round 1 Knit with B.

Round 2 *Knit 2 B, knit 2 A; repeat from * around.

Round 3 Knit 1 A, *knit 2 B, knit 2 A; repeat from * around to last stitch, knit 1 A.

Rounds 4–5 *Knit 2 A, knit 2 B; repeat from * around.

Round 6 Repeat Round 3.

Round 7 Repeat Round 2.

Round 8 Repeat Round 1.

Work 5 rounds in Bobbles Pattern as follows:

The bobbles are worked in A on a B background. Strand A across the back of work loosely, twisting A over B every third stitch to prevent puckering.

Knit 2 rounds B.

Next round *Knit 7 B, make bobble in eighth stitch as follows:

With A, (knit, purl, knit) into the same stitch, turn. Knit 3 on back side; turn and purl 3 on front side. Turn, slip 1 stitch, knit 2 stitches together, pass the slipped stitch over; repeat from * around.

Knit 2 rounds B.

Work 14 rounds in Reverse Crescent Pattern as follows:

Rounds 1–5 Knit 5 rounds with A.

Round 6 *Knit 2 A, knit 2 B; repeat from * around.

Round 7 Knit 1 B, *Knit 2 A, knit 2 B; repeat from * around to last stitch, knit 1 B.

Rounds 8–9 *Knit 2 B, knit 2 A; repeat from * around.

Round 10 Repeat round 7.

Round 11 Repeat round 6.

Rounds 12–14: Knit 3 rounds in A.

Work 4 rounds in Simple Stripes Pattern as follows:

Knit 1 round B, 1 round A, 1 round B, and 1 round A.

HEEL

The heel is twisted or twined at every stitch, a method that dates back almost two hundred years. It makes a nice padded heel that wears well and is stretchy.

Note Do NOT slip the first stitch on a row as is commonly done on other heels.

Change to smaller double-pointed needles (size 2 [2.75 mm]); with A,

knit across 12 (16, 18) stitches, turn. Purl back across 24 (32, 36) stitches. Cut B, leaving an 8" (20 cm) tail.

The remaining 24 (32, 36) stitches should be put on a holder or length of scrap yarn for the instep.

Continue to work the heel on the 24 (32, 36) stitches just purled. Rejoin B and work across: *knit 1 A, knit 1 B; repeat from * across, turn. Be sure to twist the two yarns together between stitches to create twined effect.

Next row: *Purl 1 A, purl 1 B, twining between stitches; repeat from * across, turn.

Repeat these 2 rows, creating a checked or salt-and-pepper pattern for 1¼ (1½, 1¾)" (3 [4, 4.5] cm). For the second half of the heel,

Row 1 On the right side, *purl 1 A, purl 1 B; repeat from * across, turn.

Row 2 On the wrong side, *knit 1 A, knit 1 B; repeat from * across, turn.

Repeat these 2 rows until heel measures 2½ (3, 3½)" (6 [8, 9] cm). Turn the heel as follows:

Cut B, and work only with A.

Next right side row Slip 1, knit across 11 (15, 17) stitches, knit 2

stitches together, knit 1, turn.

Row 2 Slip 1, purl 5, purl 2 together, purl 1, turn.

Row 3 Knit across to 1 stitch before the gap, knit 2 stitches together, knit 1, turn.

Row 4 Purl to 1 stitch before gap, purl 2 stitches together, purl 1, turn.

Repeat rows 3 and 4 until all the heel stitches have been worked.

HEEL GUSSET

Return to the front of the work. Divide up the stitches, putting half on a spare needle to become needle 3 with the right side gusset stitch (right side when viewing the sock from the center back). Change to B for the gusset pick-up and first rows. Knit across half the heel stitches (these stitches are now on needle 3); with another needle (needle 1), knit across the second half of the heel stitches, then pick up stitches along the first gusset. The twining makes it easy to see what stitches to pick up— only those of a single color all the way up. As you approach the stitches for the instep (on holder), pick up and knit 1 stitch from the row below to help avoid a hole. Knit the stitches on the instep holder (needle 2), pick up and knit a stitch from the row below to avoid a hole at this side of the gusset, then pick up the stitches on the second gusset, again picking up stitches of only one color. Finally, knit those stitches you put onto needle 3.

GUSSET DECREASES

Knit 2 rounds in B with no decreases. This accommodates a high arch and helps make the sock more comfortable for all.

With A, work the following decrease rounds:

Needle 1: Knit to last 2 stitches, knit 2 stitches together.

For S and L Needle 2: Knit.

For M Needle 2: Knit 1, slip 1, knit 1, pass the slipped stitch over, knit to last 3 stitches on needle, knit 2 stitches together, knit 1.

Needle 3 (all sizes): Slip 1, knit 1, pass slipped stitch over, knit to end.

Next round With A, knit even.

Continue working decrease rounds as follows and, at the same time, work Gusset Designs below.

Decrease round Needle 1: Knit to last 2 stitches, knit 2 stitches together. Needle 2: Knit. Needle 3 (all sizes): Slip 1, knit 1, pass slipped stitch over, knit to end.

Next round Knit even.

Repeat these 2 rounds until you have 48 (64, 72) stitches.

GUSSET DESIGNS

Starting from the marker at center back of the sock, on needles 1 and 3 alternate A and B stitches. On needle 2 work the Night and Day pattern as follows:

Round 1 *Knit 5 A, knit 1 B; repeat from * across. Remember to strand the B loosely and twist every 2 or 3 stitches.

Round 2 *Knit 1 B, knit 3 A, knit 2 B; repeat from * across.

Round 3 *Knit 2 B, knit 1 A, knit 3 B; repeat from * across.

Round 4 *Knit 2 A, knit 1 B, knit 3 A; repeat from * across.

Round 5 *Knit 1 A, knit 3 B, knit 2 A; repeat from * across.

Round 6 *Knit 5 B, knit 1 A; repeat from * across.

Repeat rounds 1–6 until you have completed all of the gusset decreases.

Knit 4 rounds in A, increasing 2 for medium size only to 32 stitches on needle 2.

FOOT DESIGNS

As you work these patterns, keep measuring the length of the sock foot from the back of the heel. When foot measures 6¾ (7¼, 7¾)" (17 [18.5, 19.5] cm) or 2" (5 cm) shorter than longest toe, begin toe shaping.

Note For the small sock, the last daisy pattern may have to be omitted, or switched with the checkers; for the large sock, the design bands may need an extra repeat.

Work 14 rounds in Pole Pattern as follows:

Knit 2 rounds B.

Round 1 *Knit 1 A, knit 3 B; repeat from * around.

Round 2 Repeat round 1.

Round 3 *Knit 1 A, knit 1 B; repeat from * around.

Rounds 4–5 Repeat Rounds 1 and 2.

Round 6 *Knit 1 B, knit 3 A; repeat from * around.

Round 7 Repeat round 6.

Round 8 *Knit 1 B, knit 1 A; repeat from * around.

Rounds 9–10 Repeat rounds 6 and 7.

Knit 2 rounds A.

Work 9 rounds in Taxicab Checkers Pattern as follows:

Work 4 rounds of *knit 4 B, knit 4 A; repeat from * around.

Work 4 rounds of *knit 4 A, knit 4 B; repeat from * around.

Knit 1 round A.

Work 10 rounds in Daisies Pattern as follows:

Round 1 Knit with B.

Round 2 *Knit 1 A, knit 3 B; repeat from * around.

Round 3 *Knit 1 B, knit 1 A; repeat

from * around.

Round 4 *Knit 1 A, knit 3 B; repeat from * around.

Round 5 Knit with B.

Round 6 Knit with A.

Round 7 *Knit 1 B, knit 3 A; repeat from * around.

Round 8 *Knit 1 A, knit 1 B; repeat from * around.

Round 9 *Knit 1 B, knit 3 A; repeat from * around.

Round 10 Knit with A.

TOE

Double check the number of stitches on your needles. Needles 1 and 3 should each have half as many stitches as needle 2. If necessary, redistribute the stitches so that this is true.

The toe decreases are done with a vertical striped pattern, alternating A and B and doing your best to keep the stripes matched. The toe decreases will interfere a little, but not much.

Decrease Round Needle 1: *Knit 1 A, knit 1 B; repeat from * around to

last 2 stitches, knit 2 stitches together. Needle 2: Slip 1 stitch, knit 1, pass the slipped stitch over, knit across, alternating A and B to the last 2 stitches, knit 2 stitches together. Needle 3: Slip 1 stitch, knit 1, pass the slipped stitch over, knit across.

Plain Round Knit across the 3 needles, again working on the stripes as best as possible.

Alternate these 2 rounds (decrease and plain) until only 24 (26) stitches remain. Cut A and switch to B only for the remainder of the toe. Continue to decrease until 4 stitches remain, cut yarn leaving 8" (20 cm) tail. Use a crochet hook to pull the tail through the remaining stitches; tighten, and secure yarn end. For a less pointy toe, stop decreasing when 10 stitches remain and use Kitchener stitch to finish the toe.

FINISHING

Turn sock inside out and weave in ends.

LOUNGE LIZARD SOCK

DESIGNED BY JAYA SRIKRISHNAN

KNIT/EXPERIENCED

These socks are the ultimate in keeping your tootsies toasty. They are knitted in a slip stitch pattern in worsted weight yarn, which makes them warm, durable, and cushiony.

SIZE

Women's XS (S, M, L, XL)

Finished circumference 7⅓ (8, 8⅓, 9⅔, 10)" (18.5 [20, 22, 23.5, 25.5] cm)

Finished Foot Length Approximately 8¾ (10, 10½, 10½, 11)" (22 [25.5, 26.5, 26.5, 28] cm)

MATERIALS

 LION BRAND® LION® WOOL
100% WOOL
3 OZ (85 G) 158 YD (144 M) BALL

1 (1, 2, 2, 2) balls #111 Midnight Blue (A), or color of your choice

 LION BRAND® LION® WOOL PRINT
100% WOOL
2 OZ (78 G) 143 YD (131 M) BALL

1 (1, 2, 2, 2) balls #204 Majestic Mountain (B), or color of your choice

- 2 sets size 3 (3.25 mm) double-pointed needles, *or size to obtain gauge*
- Large-eyed, blunt needle
- Stitch marker or coil-less safety pin that can be pinned to fabric

GAUGE

24 stitches and 38½ rows = 4" (10 cm) in stockinette stitch. *Be sure to check your gauge.*

PATTERN NOTES

Do not pull the yarn tight when slipping stitches. This will reduce the elasticity of the socks. All stitches are slipped as if to purl, unless indicated otherwise. Working the round to join the two tops of the sock together can be a bit awkward. Just work it slowly, making sure that all stitches are worked.

If two sets of the same size double-pointed needles are not available, the first top can be moved to a slightly smaller sized double-pointed needle after it is complete and left on the smaller needles for the joining round.

When working rounds with B in either variation of the Ribbons and Bows pattern, make sure that the yarn is loosely carried up to the current round. Twist A around B so that after the B rounds, the strand of A will hold it flat against the inside of the sock.

When adjusting the length of the foot to fit, do not work partial repeats of the Ribbons and Bows patterns. Partial repeats will leave an elongated stitch. Instead, work plain stockinette rounds for the length needed before beginning the toe shaping. Another option is to wrap the yarn fewer times in Round 2 of the Ribbons and Bows patterns: For a 6-row partial repeat, wrap the yarn twice and skip rounds 7 and 8; for a 4-row partial repeat, wrap the yarn once and skip rounds 5, 6, 7, and 8; for a 2-row partial repeat, wrap the yarn once and work rounds 1 and 2 only.

STITCH EXPLANATIONS

Ribbons and Bows Variation 1 (used on leg and top of foot)

Round 1 (B) *Slip 1 with yarn in back, knit 3; repeat from * to end of round.

Round 2 (B) *Slip 1 with yarn in back, purl 1, purl 1 wrapping yarn 3 times around needle, purl 1; repeat from * to end of round.

Round 3 (A) Knit 2, *slip 1 with yarn in back, dropping extra wraps, knit 3; rep from * to last stitch, knit 1.

Round 4 (A) Knit 2, *slip 1 with yarn in front, knit 3; repeat from * to last stitch, knit 1.

Round 5 (A) Knit 2, *slip 1 with yarn in back, knit 3; repeat from * to last stitch, knit 1.

Round 6 (A) Repeat round 4.

Round 7 (A) Repeat round 5.

Round 8 (A) Repeat round 4.

Ribbons and Bows Variation 2 (used on sole)

Round 1 (B) *Slip 1 with yarn in back, knit 3; repeat from * to end of round.

Round 2 (B) *Slip 1 with yarn in back, knit 1, knit 1 wrapping yarn 3 times around needle, knit 1; repeat from * to end of round.

Round 3 (A) Knit 2, *slip 1 with yarn in back dropping extra wraps, knit 3; repeat from * to last stitch, knit 1.

Round 4 (A) Knit 2, *slip 1 with yarn in front, knit 3; repeat from * to last stitch, knit 1.

Round 5 (A) Knit 2, *slip 1 with yarn in back, knit 3; repeat from * to last stitch, knit 1.

Round 6 (A) Repeat round 4.

Round 7 (A) Repeat round 5.

Round 8 (A) Repeat round 4.

Eye of Partridge (used on heel flap)

Row 1 (B) *Slip 1, knit 1; repeat from * to end or row.

Row 2 (B) Slip 1, purl to end of row.

Row 3 (A) Slip 1, *slip 1, knit 1; repeat from * to last stitch from end, knit 1.

Row 4 (A) Slip 1, purl to end of row.

CUFF

With B, cast on 44 (48, 52, 56, 60) stitches. Join in the round, being careful not to twist. Mark beginning of round with a stitch marker pinned below the needle. Knit 10 rounds.

Next 2 rounds (1 x 1 rib) *Knit 1, purl 1, repeat from * to end of round.

Knit 5 rounds. Do not cut yarn. Leave on needles (or transfer to slightly smaller needles) and set aside.

With A, cast on 44 (48, 52, 56, 60) stitches. Work as for B cuff to the end of the two 1 x 1 rib rounds. Carefully insert the B cuff inside the tube of the A cuff, so that the A tube is on the outside. Holding the needles with the two cuffs parallel to each other, join the two cuffs together by inserting the right needle tip into the first stitch of the A cuff, then the first stitch of the B cuff, and knitting through both stitches with A. Continue knitting all the way around in this manner, joining the two cuffs. Set aside the second set of double-pointed needles.

Work 5 full repeats of Ribbons and Bows Variation 1 Pattern (or full repeats to reach desired length).

HEEL FLAP

Row 1 Using A, knit 11 (12, 13, 14, 15), weaving B above and below the A working yarn on the reverse side of the sock. Slip 11 (12, 13, 14, 15) stitches from each side of the round marker to a single needle—

22 (24, 26, 28, 30) stitches total form the heel flap. Set aside the other 22 (24, 26, 28, 30) stitches for the instep. Continue on a right side row.

Row 2 (A) Slip 1, purl to end. Do not turn work. Slide stitches back to other end of the needle.

Row 3 (B) Purl to end, turn. Beginning with row 3 of the Eye of Partridge Pattern (page 70), work 20 (22, 24, 26, 28) rows.

TURN HEEL

Using B only,

Row 1 Slip 1, knit 12 (13, 14, 15, 16), slip slip knit, knit 1, turn (leave remaining stitches unworked on left needle).

Row 2 Slip 1, purl 5, purl 2 stitches together, purl 1, turn.

Row 3 Slip 1, knit 6, slip slip knit, knit 1, turn.

Row 4 Slip 1, purl 7, purl 2 stitches together, purl 1, turn.

Continue working 1 more stitch on each row until all stitches have been worked.

GUSSET

Using B, knit across the heel stitches, pick up and knit 11 (12, 13, 14, 15) stitches along the left side of the heel flap, work round 1 of Ribbons and Bows Variation 1 on the 22 (24, 26, 28, 30) stitches of the instep, pick up and knit 11 (12, 13, 14, 15) stitches along the right side of the heel flap. Weaving A over and under the B working yarn, knit to the center of the heel—58, (62, 68, 72, 78) stitches. Mark the new beginning of the round in the center of the sole stitches.

Using the colors indicated for the Ribbons and Bows Variation 1, work gusset as follows:

Round 1 Knit to 3 stitches before the end of the gusset, slip slip knit, knit 1, work stitch pattern on instep, knit 1, knit 2 stitches together, knit to end of round.

Round 2 Knit to end of gusset, work pattern on instep, knit to end of round.

Repeat these 2 rounds until 44 (48, 52, 56, 60) stitches are left on needles. Round 8 of Ribbons and Bows Variation 1 should be the last round worked.

FOOT

Continue knitting, working Ribbons and Bows Variation 2 on the sole stitches and Ribbons and Bows Variation 1 on the top of the foot until 5 (6, 6, 6, 6) repeats of pattern have been worked or foot is the desired length (should reach to the middle joint of the big toe). Break A. Toe is worked in B only.

SHAPE TOE

Round 1 Knit to 3 stitches before side of foot, slip slip knit, knit 1, knit 1, knit 2 stitches together, knit to 3 stitches before other side of foot, slip slip knit, knit 1, knit 1, knit 2 stitches together, knit to end of round.

Round 2 Knit all stitches.

Repeat these 2 rounds until 20 (24, 24, 28, 28) stitches are left on needles. Knit 5 (6, 6, 7, 7) stitches to get the yarn to the side of the foot.

FINISHING

Cut B, leaving sufficient length to graft toe. Graft toe using Kitchener stitch. Weave in ends and block.

FAIR ISLE HEART SOCKS

DESIGNED BY CARLA STURGIS
KNIT/INTERMEDIATE

Just right for Valentine's Day (or anytime, really!), these heart socks are knit using Fair Isle stranding techniques.

SIZE

Women's M/L
Finished measurements 10" long x 11" around ball of foot (25.4 x 27.9 cm)

MATERIALS

 LION BRAND® LION® WOOL
100% WOOL
3 OZ (85 G) 158 YD (144 M) BALL

1 ball #113 Scarlet (A) and 2 balls #099 Winter White (B), or colors of your choice
• 1 set of 4 size 5 (3.75 mm) double-pointed needles, *or size to obtain gauge*
• Large-eyed, blunt needle

GAUGE

20 stitches = 4" (10 cm).
Be sure to check your gauge.

SOCK

Using A, cast on 48 stitches onto needle 1. While knitting the stitches, divide over 3 needles as follows: 12/24/12. Work in knit 2, purl 2 rib for 3 rows. Change to B and continue with ribbing for an additional 10 rows (top band). Remember to pull the first stitch on each needle tightly or there will be a ladder-like gap!

CUFF

Change to A and knit 1 round. Change to B and work 6 rounds. You are now ready to work 2-handed Fair Isle hearts into the cuff of the sock. Follow Chart 1 working from right to left and repeating

chart 4 times around for pattern. Work 6 rounds of stockinette stitch in B.
Work 1 round of stockinette stitch in A.
Work 8 rounds of stockinette stitch in B.

DIVIDE FOR HEEL

Knit across needle 1 so that stitches from needles 1 and 3 are now on the same needle. Purl back across these same stitches. You now have 2 needles, each with 24 stitches. This needle of stitches will be worked for the heel as follows: Work 10 rows back and forth in stockinette stitch using B. Now use Chart 2 to knit the heart into the center of the heel flap. Work 3 rows of stockinette stitch in B.

TURN HEEL

Row 1 Knit half of the stitches across heel flap, plus 1, then knit 2 stitches together, knit 1, turn.

Row 2 Purl 5, purl 2 stitches together, purl 1, turn.

Row 3 Knit to 1 stitch before gap, knit 2 stitches together (you are knitting 1 stitch before the gap and 1 stitch after the gap together), knit 1, turn.

Row 4 Purl to one stitch before gap, purl 2 stitches together, purl 1, turn.

Repeat rows 3 and 4 until no stitches remain on either end of needle (forms the cup of the heel), ending with a wrong side row. Turn.

Next row Knit to end. Pick up and knit 11 stitches evenly along first side of heel. Using a second needle knit across the 24 stitches of instep. Using a third needle pick up and knit 11 stitches evenly along second side of heel and knit across half the stitches from end of needle 1. Move remaining stitches to the end of what will now be needle 1.

GUSSET

Round 1 Knit.

Round 2 Knit to last 3 stitches on first needle, knit 2 stitches together, knit 1, knit across stitches on needle 2, continuing in pattern established (knit 3, purl 1). On needle 3, knit 1, slip 1, knit 1, pass slipped stitch over, knit to end.

Repeat the last 2 rounds until 48 stitches remain.

Work 10 rounds in stockinette stitch. Change to A and work 1 round. Change back to B yarn and work 4 rounds.

Next 8 rounds Knit Chart 2 with A into the next 8 rounds on the center 8 stitches of needle 2. Work 4 rounds in B. Work 1 round in A. Work 10 rounds in B, or until desired length of sock minus 1½" (3.8 cm).

TOE

Change to A.

Round 1 Knit.

Round 2 Knit to last 3 stitches on needle 1, knit 2 stitches together, knit 1; on needle 2 knit 1, slip 1, knit 1, pass the slipped stitch over, knit to last 3 stitches on needle, knit 2 stitches together, knit 1; on needle 3, knit 1, slip 1, knit 1, pass the slipped stitch over, knit to end.

Repeat the last 2 rounds until 24 stitches remain, then decrease as before on every round until 20 stitches remain, moving the 4 stitches on needle 3 to needle 1 so there are 8 stitches on 2 needles. Cut yarn, leaving approximately 12" (30.5 cm) for sewing toe. Weave the 2 sets of 10 stitches together using Kitchener stitch. Sew in ends.

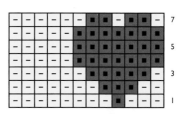

Chart 1

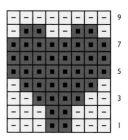

Chart 2

■ contrast color

– main color

4.
STITCH PATTERNS

Stitch patterns add texture and visual interest to even the plainest single-color socks, and they're fun to work, too. All the socks in this chapter were designed with coziness in mind, so the stitchwork won't get in the way of fit and comfort.

SUMMER WAVE SOCKS

DESIGNED BY LAURA ANDERSSON
KNIT/BEGINNER

This is a fun shortie for summer with an easy and interesting stitch pattern. The fabric is super soft!

SIZE

Women's S (M, L)

Sample shown 9" long x 11" around ball of foot (22.9 x 27.9 cm)

MATERIALS

 LION BRAND® MICROSPUN 100% MICROFIBER ACRYLIC 2½ OZ (70 G) 168 YD (154 M) BALL

2 balls #103 Coral, or color of your choice

- Double-pointed needles in size 3 (3.25 mm) for leg and size 2 (2.75 mm) for heel and foot, *or size to obtain gauge*
- Large-eyed, blunt needle or crochet hook

GAUGE

32 stitches = 4" (10 cm) measured in stockinette stitch.
Be sure to check your gauge.

STITCH EXPLANATION

Peachy Keen Stitch Pattern
(multiple of 15 stitches)

Round 1 Knit 2, (knit 2 stitches together) twice, knit 5, (knit into front and back of next stitch) twice, knit 2.

Round 2 Knit all stitches.

TOP

Cast on 45 (60, 75) stitches using size 3 needles and the following method: Cast on 1 stitch, leaving an approximately 8" (20 cm) tail. Knit into this first stitch, but do NOT move to the right needle as usual; instead place the stitch on the end of the left needle. Knit into this stitch and place the new loop on the end of the left needle. Continue knitting into the last stitch and slipping the new loop to the left needle until the required number is reached. This cast-on has a very slight stretch, so if you knit tightly you may wish to cast on with larger needles.

Join, being careful not to twist. Place marker.

Work in Peachy Keen Stitch Pattern for 3–4" (7.5–10 cm) or desired length. Increase 1 (0, 1), to a final stitch count of 46 (60, 76). Work ½" (1.3 cm) of knit 1, purl 1 rib. This adds fit and shaping to your ankle and the instep.

HEEL FLAP

The heel is worked across roughly half of the total stitches—23 (30, 38).

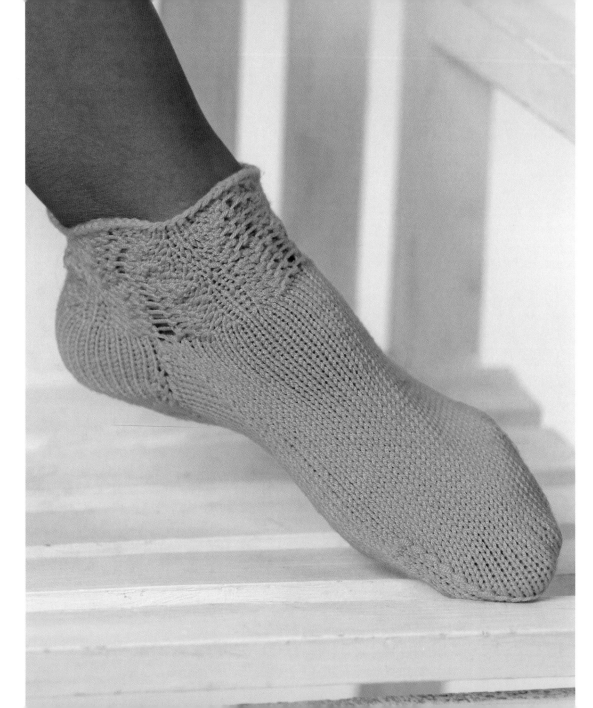

Row 1 Knit 12 (15, 19), turn.

Row 2 Purl 23 (30, 38).

Place remaining 23 (30, 38) stitches on a piece of waste yarn or stitch holder.

All right side rows *Slip 1, knit 1; repeat from * across, turn.

All wrong side rows Slip 1, purl across, turn.

Repeat these 2 rows until your heel is 2¾ (3, 3¼)" (7 [7.5, 8] cm) from start.

TURN HEEL

Row 1 Slip 1, knit 12 (15, 19), knit 2, knit 2 stitches together, knit 1, turn.

Row 2 (WS) Slip 1, purl 5, purl 2 stitches together, purl 1, turn. Continue working in this manner, knitting on the right side and purling on the wrong side to the gap and then decrease 1 (knit 2 stitches together or purl 2 stitches together), work 1, turn. Repeat until all stitches are worked. End on a wrong side row.

GUSSET

Round 1 Slip 1 and knit across half of the stitches on the needle; these will join needle 3 for right side of heel. With a new needle, which will be needle 1, knit across the remaining stitches on the first needle. Going down the side, pick up and knit 1 stitch for each slipped stitch on the edge of heel flap, plus an extra at the top of instep.

Round 2 Knit.

Begin to decrease gussets as follows:

Round 3 Needle 1: * Knit 2, purl 2; repeat from * to within 2 stitches of end of needle, knit 2 stitches together; needle 2: knit in pattern across instep; needle 3: slip 1, knit 1, pass slipped stitch over, *knit 2, purl 2; repeat from * to end.

Round 4 Work in pattern (needles 1 and 3 are knit 2, purl 2 rib and needle 2 is the Peachy Keen Pattern). Repeat these 2 rounds until you are back to the original number of stitches.

FOOT

Work stockinette stitch until sock measures 1.5" (4 cm) less than the total length of your foot.

TOE

You should have at least half the stitches on needle 2 and one-quarter of the stitches on each of needles 1 and 3. Any extra stitches go onto needle 2.

Round 1 Knit across needle 1 to last 2 stitches, knit 2 stitches together; needle 2: Slip 1, knit 1, pass the slipped stitch over, knit to last 2 stitches, knit 2 stitches together; needle 3: Slip 1, knit 1, pass the slipped stitch over, and knit to end.

Round 2 Knit all stitches.

Work these 2 rounds until you have only 8 (10, 12) stitches remaining and close the toe with Kitchener stitch.

FINISHING

Weave in all ends and block.

MOSS ON THE MOUNTAIN SOCKS

DESIGNED BY JUDY SUMNER
KNIT/INTERMEDIATE

Let the yarn do the work in these beautifully textured socks!

SIZE
Women's M
Sample shown 9" long x 7" around ball of foot (22.9 x 17.8 cm)

MATERIALS
 LION BRAND® LION® WOOL PRINTS
100% WOOL
2¾ OZ (78 G) 143 YD (131 M) BALL

2 balls #204 Majestic Mountain, or color of your choice

- Set of 5 size 4 (3.5 mm) double-pointed needles, *or size to obtain gauge*
- Large-eyed, blunt needle

GAUGE
24 stitches and 34 rows= 4" (10 cm) in stockinette stitch.
Be sure to check your gauge.

STITCH EXPLANATIONS
tbl Through back loop.
Pass Slipped Stitch Over Pass slipped stitch over the last stitch knit.

STITCH PATTERN
(10 stitch repeat)
Round 1 *(Purl 1, knit 1) twice, yarn over, knit 2 stitches together tbl, knit 1, knit 2 stitches together, yarn over, knit 1; repeat from * to end of round.
Rounds 2 and 4 *(Knit 1, purl 1) twice, knit 5, purl 1; repeat from * to end of round.
Round 3 *(Purl 1, knit 1) twice, knit 1, yarn over, slip 1, knit 2 sitches together, pass the slipped stitch over, yarn over, knit 2; repeat from * to end of round.

CUFF
Cast on 40 stitches and divide evenly among four needles. Work knit 1, purl 1 rib for 1½" (4 cm). Change to pattern stitch and work until cuff measures 6" (15 cm), or desired length, ending with round 4.

HEEL FLAP
Row 1 Knit across needle 1, turn.
Row 2 Slip 1, then purl across needles 1 and 4. Place these 20 stitches on one needle for heel flap.
Row 3 *Slip 1, knit 1; repeat from * to end of row.
Row 4 Slip 1, purl to end of row. Repeat the last 2 rows until 21 rows are completed, ending with a purl row.

TURN HEEL

Row 1 Slip 1, knit 11, knit 2 stitches together tbl, knit 1, turn.

Row 2 Slip 1, purl 5, purl 2 stitches together, purl 1, turn.

Row 3 Slip 1, knit 6, knit 2 stitches together tbl, knit 1, turn.

Row 4 Slip 1, purl 7, purl 2 stitches together, purl 1, turn.

Continue in this manner, working 1 more stitch before decrease on each row until 12 stitches remain. Knit to end.

GUSSET

Round 1 Pick up 11 stitches along the side of the heel flap, make 1 stitch in loop between heel flap and instep needle, knit across two instep needles, make 1 stitch in loop between instep needle and heel flap, pick up 11 stitches along other side of heel flap.

Divide heel stitches between needles 1 and 4.

Work 1 round, knitting the stitch at each edge of the heel flap together with the adjacent instep stitch, and working in stockinette stitch on the instep.

Decrease Round Knit to 3 stitches from end of first needle, slip 1, knit 1, pass slipped stitch over, knit 1, knit instep stitches, knit 1, knit 2 stitches together, knit to end of round.

Work one round even.

Repeat these two rounds until 20 heel stitches remain.

FOOT

Work as established until foot length is 1½" (4 cm) less than desired length from back of heel.

TOE

Decrease Round Work until 3 stitches remain on needle 1, knit 2 stitches together tbl, knit 1, knit 1, knit 2 stitches together, knit remaining stitches on needle 2, knit across needle 3 until 3 stitches remain, knit 2 stitches together tbl, knit 1, knit 1, knit 2 stitches together, knit to end on needle 4.

Knit 1 row.

Repeat these 2 rows until 4 stitches remain on each needle.

FINISHING

Graft toe. Weave in ends and block.

PUMPKIN SLIP STITCH SOCK

DESIGNED BY MARYLOU EGAN

KNIT/INTERMEDIATE

Bright socks get an extra punch of color with the addition of multi-colored yarn. Try several different yarn combinations, if you dare.

SIZE

Adult M (L, XL)

The sizing is based on the width of the foot. Medium generally fits a woman's foot or a narrow man's foot, Large fits a wider foot or an average man's foot, Extra Large fits a wide man's foot.

Sample shown 10" long x 10" around ball of foot (25 x 25 cm)

MATERIALS

 LION BRAND® LION® WOOL
100% WOOL

3 OZ (85 G) 158 YD (144 M) BALL

1 ball #133 Pumpkin (A), or color of your choice

 LION BRAND® LION® WOOL PRINTS (B)
100% WOOL

2 OZ (78 G) 143 YD (131 M) BALL

1 ball #133 Autumn Sunset, or colors of your choice

- Reinforcing yarn for heel and toe (optional)
- Set of 5 size 5 (3.75 mm) double-pointed needles, *or size to obtain gauge*
- Set of 5 size 3 (3.25 mm) double-pointed needles, *or size to obtain gauge*
- Large-eyed, blunt needle

GAUGE

22 stitches and 30 rows over 4" (10 cm) over stockinette.

Be sure to check your gauge.

LEG

With A, using larger needles, cast on 48 (52, 56) stitches. Join, being careful not to twist. Switch to smaller needles. Divide stitches so the first needle has 12 (12, 16), the second needle has 24 (28, 24), and the third needle has 12 (12, 16). Work around in knit 2, purl 2 ribbing 14 rounds.

Knit 1 round, increasing 0 (2, 4) stitches evenly—48 (54, 60) stitches.

Begin working in Slip Stitch Pattern.

SLIP STITCH PATTERN

Round 1 (A) Knit 2, *slip 1, knit 5, repeat from * around, ending with knit 3.

Round 2 (A) Repeat round 1.

Round 3 (B) *Knit 5, slip 1, repeat from * around.

Round 4 (B) *Purl 5, slip 1 with yarn in back; repeat from * around. Repeat these 4 rounds for 6" (15 cm), or until sock is desired length.

Finish with round 1.

At beginning of next round, knit 12 (13, 15) stitches, turn work, slip 1, purl 23 (25, 29). These 24 (26, 30) purled stitches will be worked back and forth for the heel flap. Divide instep stitches over 2 needles.

HEEL FLAP

Break B and continue knitting heel flap in A. Add reinforcing yarn here, if desired.

Row 1 Slip 1, knit across.

Row 2 Slip 1, purl across.

Repeat these 2 rows until 21 rows have been completed, ending with a right side row.

TURN HEEL

Row 1 Purl 14 (15, 17), purl 2 stitches together, purl 1, turn.

Row 2 Slip 1, knit 5, knit 2 stitches together, knit 1, turn.

Row 3 Slip 1, purl 6, purl 2 stiches together, purl 1, turn.

Row 4 Slip 1, knit 7, knit 2 stitches together, knit 1, turn.

Repeat the last 2 rows, continuing to work 1 more stitch in the center section of each row, until all stitches have been worked and there are 14 (16, 18) stitches remaining.

Break reinforcing yarn.

GUSSET

With the same needle, pick up 11 stitches along the right side of the heel.

Pick up and twist the yarn in the gap between the heel flap and the first instep needle. Put this stitch on the needle with the heel flap stitches.

With one needle, work across all instep stitches, keeping them in pattern stitch (round 2 of pattern). With empty needle, pick up and twist the yarn in the gap between the instep needle and the heel flap. With the same needle, pick up 11 stitches along the left side of heel. Knit half of heel stitches from the first needle.

The round now begins in the middle of the heel.

Round 1 Knit.

Round 2 Knit until 3 stitches from the end of needle 1, knit 2 stitches together, knit 1. Work knit 1, purl 1 across instep needle stitches. At the beginning of needle 3, knit 1, slip slip knit, knit to end.

Continue working these 2 rounds until there are 48 (54, 60) stitches remaining.

FOOT

Work as established, with the pattern stitch on the instep, and the other two needles in stockinette, until foot is about 1½" (4 cm) from desired length.

TOE

Round 1 Knit until 3 stitches from the end of needle 1, knit 2 stitches together, knit 1; knit 1, slip slip knit, knit to 3 stitches from end of needle 2, knit 2 stitches together, knit 1; knit 1, slip slip knit, knit to end of needle 3.

Round 2 Knit.

Repeat these 2 rounds until there are 24 (24, 28) stitches remaining. Break yarn, leaving a 12" (30.5 cm) tail. Divide stitches over two needles, 12 (12, 14) stitches on each needle. Graft remaining stitches. Weave in ends and block.

THE FOREST AND THE TREES SOCKS

DESIGNED BY MARIE DECHATELAINE

KNIT/INTERMEDIATE

The forestlike colors of the yarn inspired a subtle tree design on the knit panels of a wide rib pattern. The ribs continue down the heel, making them perfect for wearing with clogs. The sole is in reverse stockinette with smooth toe decreases for comfort. The instructions are written using the Magic Loop method (see page 12), but can easily be modified for 2 circular needles or double-pointed needles (see pages 11 and 12). Do you see the forest or the trees?

SIZE

Women's M (Men's M)

Sample shown 9½" long x 9" around ball of foot (24 x 23 cm) for women's; 12" x 11" (30.5 x 28 cm) for men's

MATERIALS

 LION BRAND® LION® WOOL-EASE®

80% ACRYLIC, 20% WOOL

2½ OZ (70 G) 162 YD (146 M) BALL

2 (3) balls #232 Wood, or color of your choice

- Size 3 (3.25 mm) 40"(101.5 cm) circular needle, *or size to obtain gauge*
- Stitch markers
- Large-eyed, blunt needle

GAUGE

24 stitches and 34 rows = 4" (10 cm) in stockinette stitch. *Be sure to check your gauge.*

NOTE

When a purl stitch is at the beginning of a side, be sure to pull the yarn firmly to avoid ladders.

STITCH PATTERNS

Pattern A *Knit 7, purl 5 (7); repeat from * to end for 9 rounds in the rib pattern.

Pattern B *Work chart in place of Knit 7 in Pattern A, purl 5 (7); repeat from * to end for 11 rounds.

CUFF

Cast on 48 (56) stitches and join, being careful not to twist. Work in knit 2, purl 2 rib for 1½" (4 cm), about 13 rounds.

LEG

Women's Work Patterns A and B twice, then 8 rows of Pattern A.

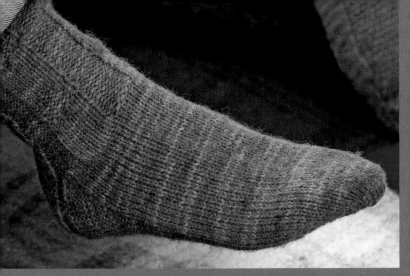

Men's Work Patterns A and B a total of three times each, ending with round 9 on last repeat of Pattern B.

HEEL FLAP

Women's Knit 7, purl 5, knit 7, purl 2, move next 3 stitches to cable, turn.

On next side, purl 3, knit 7, purl 5, knit 7, purl 3, move next 2 stitches to cable in order to move them to other side—23 heel stitches on needle end 1, 25 instep stitches on needle end 2.

Men's Continuing round 10 of pattern B, work to last 4 stitches on first side, move these 4 stitches to cable and switch needle ends. Work across second side to last 3 stitches. Move these 3 stitches to cable and switch ends—27 heel stitches on needle end 1, 29 instep stitches on needle end 2.

Both sizes Begin working back and forth across heel stitches on needle end 1.

Row 1 (RS) Slip 1 purlwise with yarn in front, purl 1 (2), knit 7 (7), purl 5 (7), knit 7 (7), purl 2 (3), turn.

Row 2 Slip 1 purlwise with yarn in back, knit 1, *slip 1 with yarn in front, purl 1; repeat from * 3 (4) times. Slip 1 with yarn in front, *knit 1, slip 1 with yarn in front; repeat from * 2 (3) times. Knit 1, *slip 1 with yarn in front, purl 1;

repeat from * 3 (4) times. Slip 1 with yarn in front, knit 2, turn. Repeat rows 1 and 2 until heel flap is 22 (24) rows long or your required length. End with a wrong side row.

TURN HEEL

Slip the first stitch of each row purlwise with yarn in front.

Row 1 Slip 1, purl 13 (15), purl 2 stitches together, purl 1, turn.

Row 2 Slip 1, knit 6, knit 2 stitches together, knit 1, turn.

Row 3 Slip 1, purl to 1 stitch before gap, purl 2 stitches together, purl 1, turn.

Row 4 Slip 1, knit to 1 stitch before gap, knit 2 stitches together, knit 1, turn.

Repeat rows 3 and 4 until all stitches of the heel are used—15 (17) stitches.

GUSSET

Return to working in rounds. Purl 8 (9) across heel, move to cable, purl 7 (8) more heel stitches, pick up and purl 1 stitch in each loop along edge of heel flap, pick up loop in gap between instep and gusset, twist and purl. Place

marker, change needle ends, knit 12 (15) stitches across instep, move stitches to cable and change needle ends, knit 13 (14) across rest of instep, place marker, pick up loop in gap between instep and gusset, twist and purl stitch, pick up and purl stitches along edge of flap, purl 7 (9) heel stitches—12 heel and gusset stitches and 12 instep stitches on needle end 1, 12 instep and gusset stitches and 12 heel stitches on needle end 2. Rounds begin at center of heel.

Decrease Round Purl heel stitches, purl across gusset to 2 stitches before marker, slip slip knit, slip marker, knit across instep, slip marker, knit 2 stitches together, purl to end of round.

Repeat decrease round until 48 (56) stitches remain—23 (27) purl stitches on needle end 1, 25 (29) knit stitches on needle end 2.

FOOT

Continuing to work in rounds, knit the instep and purl the sole until foot measures 2" (2¼") [5 (5.75) cm] less than desired length. On last round, move 2nd marker 1 stitch into stockinette stitch (instep) panel—24 (28) stitches between markers.

TOE

Round 1 (Decrease Round) Purl to 2 stitches before marker, slip slip knit, slip marker, knit 2 stiches together, knit to 2 stitches before marker, slip slip knit, slip marker, knit 2 stitches together, purl to end of round.

Round 2 Work even.
Round 3 Work even.

Work last 3 rounds 2 (3) times, then rounds 1 and 2, until 24 (28) stitches remain. Repeat round 1 until 12 (16) stitches remain.

Purl 1 (2), knit 1, move to cable, remove marker, slip 3 (5), change needle ends, slip 3, move stitches to cable, remove marker.

Adjust needles so open points of both needles are at the side with the yarn attached. Graft remaining stitches. Weave in ends and block.

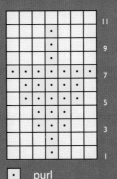

· purl

knit

5.
SPECIAL OCCASIONS

Special occasions aren't limited to holidays, although we've got you covered in that department with Christmas stockings. Even a pedicure can be a special occasion if you're taking time out for yourself.

TOELESS PEDICURE SOCK

DESIGNED BY ANDI SMITH FOR KNITBRIT

KNIT/EASY

Whether you like to wiggle your toes or you're actually using these for their intended purpose, you'll love these fantastic pedicure socks.

SIZE

Women's S/M
Sample shown 6½" long x 7" around ball of foot (16.5 x 17.8 cm)

MATERIALS

 LION BRAND® MICROSPUN
100% MICROFIBER ACRYLIC
2½ OZ (70 G) 168 YD (154 M) BALL

2 balls #100 Lily White, or color of your choice

- Set of size 3 (3.25 mm) double-pointed needles, *or size to obtain gauge*
- Large-eyed, blunt needle

GAUGE

32 stitches = 4" (10 cm) measured in stockinette stitch.
Be sure to check your gauge.

STITCH EXPLANATIONS

Lace Pattern
Round 1 (RS) *Purl 2, knit 5; repeat to end.
Round 2 *Knit 2, purl 5; repeat to end.
Round 3 *Purl 2, knit 2 stitches together, yarn over, knit 1, yarn over, slip slip knit; repeat to end.
Round 4 Repeat row 2.

CUFF

Cast on 42 stitches and divide among three needles—14 on each needle.
Work 2 of knit 1, purl 1 rib, working in the round.
Work 4" (10 cm) of lace pattern ending with either a second or fourth lace pattern row.

HEEL FLAP

Row 1 *Slip 1, knit 1; repeat from * 10 times, turn—20 stitches.

Row 2 Slip 1, purl to end.
Continue working on these 20 stitches for 21 more rows.

TURN HEEL

Row 24 Slip 1, purl 12, purl 2 stitches together, purl 1, turn.
Row 25 Slip 1, knit 5, knit 2 stitches together, knit 1, turn.
Row 26 Slip 1, purl 6, purl 2 stitches together, purl 1, turn.
Row 27 Slip 1, knit 7, knit 2 stiches together, knit 1, turn.
Row 28 Slip 1, purl 8, purl 2 stitches together, purl 1, turn.
Continue in this manner until all heel stitches have been worked, ending with 12 stitches. Do not turn.
Pick up 11 stitches along left heel edge, work pattern across instep stitches, pick up 11 stitches along right heel edge, and work 6 stitches of heel—54 stitches.

HEEL GUSSET

Round 1 Knit to 3 stitches before instep stitches, knit 2 stitches together, knit 1, work in pattern across instep stitches, knit 1, slip slip knit, knit to end—52 stitches. Repeat round 1 until there are 42 stitches remaining.

FOOT

Reestablish lace pattern around and work foot until it is 2½" (6 cm) shorter than your foot. Work 1" (2.5 cm) of knit 1, purl 1 rib. Bind off in pattern and weave in loose ends.

TABI SOCKS

DESIGNED BY ANDI SMITH FOR KNITBRIT
KNIT/INTERMEDIATE

Tabi socks originated in Japan, where even construction workers wear split-toe socks. These look great around the house or with sandals and add just a little more wiggle room for your toes.

SIZE
Women's M
Sample shown 9" long x 9" around ball of foot (22.9 x 22.9 cm)

MATERIALS

 LION BRAND® LION® WOOL
100% WOOL
3 OZ (85 G) 158 YD (144 M) BALL

2 balls #178 Dark Teal, or color of your choice

- Size 4 (3.5 mm) double-pointed needles, *or size to obtain gauge*
- Stitch holder
- Large-eyed blunt needle

GAUGE
22 stitches = 4" (10 cm) in stockinette stitch

STITCH EXPLANATION
tw2 (Twist 2) Knit the second stitch on the left-hand needle without taking it off the needle, then knit the first stitch on the left-hand needle, taking both stitches off the needle at the same time.

LEFT SOCK
Cast on 48 stitches and divide evenly over 4 needles—12 stitches on each needle.
Round 1 *Purl 1, knit 2; repeat from * to end.
Round 2 *Purl 1, tw2; repeat from * to end.
These two rows form pattern.
Work 4" (10 cm) or to length desired.

HEEL FLAP
Using only stitches from first two needles (24 stitches):

Row 1 Slip 1, knit 1, repeat to end.
Row 2 Slip 1, purl to end.
Repeat these rows until there are 11 slipped stitches on both sides of the heel.

TURN HEEL
Row 1 Slip 1, knit 13, slip slip knit, knit 1, turn.
Row 2 Slip 1, purl 5, purl 2 stitches together, purl 1, turn.
Row 3 Slip 1, knit 6, slip slip knit, knit 1, turn.
Row 4 Slip 1, purl 7, purl 2 stitches together, purl 1, turn.
Row 5 Slip 1, knit 8, slip slip knit, knit 1, turn.
Row 6 Slip 1, purl 9, purl 2 stitches together, purl 1, turn.
Row 7 Slip 1, knit 10, slip slip knit, knit 1, turn.
Row 8 Slip 1, purl 11, purl 2 stitches together, purl 1—14 stitches.

Row 9 Knit 14, pick up and knit 11 stitches along heel flap, work the instep stitches in pattern, pick up and knit 11 stitches along the other side of the heel flap, and work 7 stitches from the heel (place the last heel flap and 7 heel stitches onto needle 4).

Stitches should be distributed thus: 18, 12, 12, 18—60 stitches total.

GUSSET

Round 1 On needle 1, knit to last 3 stitches, knit 2 stitches together, knit 1. On needles 2 and 3, work in pattern. On needle 4, knit 1, slip slip knit, knit to end: 17, 12, 12, 17—58 total stitches.

Round 2 Knit on needles 1 and 4, work in pattern on needles 2 and 3. Repeat rounds 1 and 2 until 48 stitches remain—12 stitches on each needle.

Work in established pattern until foot measures approximately 8" (20 cm) or reaches bottom of big toe.

DIVIDE FOR TOE

Round 1 Knit 4, slip remaining 8 stitches and first 8 stitches from needle 2 onto holder, knit remaining 4 stitches on needle 2 plus

TABI SOCKS

stitches on needles 3 and 4—32 stitches total.

Redistribute stitches on needles so there are 8 on each needle beginning with stitches from the toe split (these are now on needle 1). Knit 3 rounds.

SHAPE TOES

Round 1 Knit needle 1, on needle 2, knit to last 3 stitches, slip slip knit, knit 1, on needle 3, knit 1, knit 2 stitches together, knit to end, knit needle 4—30 stitches.

Repeat round 1 three times—24 stitches.

Round 5 Knit.

Round 6 Repeat round 1—22 stitches.

Repeat rounds 5 and 6—20 stitches.

Round 9 Knit 1, knit 2 stitches together, knit to last 3 stitches on needle 4, slip slip knit, knit 1—18 stitches.

Bind off.

BIG TOE

Pick up 16 stitches along base of toe, increasing 1 stitch at beginning and end—18 stitches.

Knit 12 rounds.

Round 13 (Knit 1, slip slip knit, knit 1, knit 2 stitches together) to end. Cut yarn, weave yarn through remaining stitches, pull tightly and fasten off.

RIGHT SOCK

Work as for left sock through gusset, then divide for toe:

Round 1 Knit needles 1 and 2, knit 4 stitches on needle 3, place next 8 stitches on holder along with following 8 stitches from needle 4, knit remaining 4 stitches from needle 4—32 stitches.

Redistribute stitches on needles so there are 8 stitches on each needle as follows, 4 stitches from needle 1 onto needle 4, 4 stitches from needle 2 onto the beginning of needle 3.

Knit 3 rounds.

SHAPE TOES

Round 1 Knit needle 1, knit needle 2, on needle 3, knit to last 3 stitches, slip slip knit, knit 1, on needle 4, knit 1, knit 2 stitches together, knit to end—30 stitches.

Repeat round 1 three times—24 stitches.

Round 5 Knit.

Round 6 Repeat round 1—22 stitches.

Repeat rounds 5 and 6—20 stitches.

Round 9 Knit 1, knit 2 stitches together, knit to last 3 stitches on needle 4, slip slip knit, knit 1—18 stitches.

Bind off.

BIG TOE

Pick up 16 stitches along base of toe, increase 1 stitch at beginning and end—18 stitches.

Knit 12 rounds.

Next Round (Knit 1, slip slip knit, knit 1, knit 2 stitches together) to end.

Cut yarn, weave yarn through remaining stitches, pull tightly, and fasten off.

FINISHING

To finish tabi socks, turn inside out and sew toe seam together. Weave in ends.

MOCCASIN SLIPPERS

DESIGNED BY KATE ATHERLEY

KNIT/EASY

These slippers are cushy and perfect for a night in with popcorn. They'll keep your toes warm no matter how cold it is outside.

SIZE

Women's S (L)

Sample Shown 9.5" long x 9" around ball of foot (24.1 x 22.9 cm)

MATERIALS

 LION BRAND® WOOL-EASE® THICK & QUICK®
80% ACRYLIC, 20% WOOL
6 OZ (170 G) 108 YD (98 M) BALL

1 ball each #122 Taupe (A) and #112 Raspberry (B), or colors of your choice

- 1 pair size 13 (9 mm) straight needles, *or size to obtain gauge*
- 1 set size 11 (8 mm) double-pointed needles, *or size to obtain gauge*
- Size J-10 (6 mm) hook
- Large-eyed, blunt needle

GAUGE

9 stitches and 13 rows = 4" (10 cm) in stockinette stitch using size 13 (9 mm) needles.
Be sure to check gauge.

HEEL

Using A, cast 6 stitches onto straight needles. Work flat in stockinette stitch (knit right side row, purl wrong side row) for 2½" (3") [6 (7.5 cm)].

FOOT

Cast on 4 (5) stitches at beginning of next 2 rows—14 (16) stitches. Work even in stockinette stitch until piece measures 6½ (8)" [16 (20 cm)] from cast-on edge.

SHAPE TOE

Continuing in stockinette stitch, knit 2 stitches together at each end of the row, every other row, until 6 stitches remain.

TOE FLAP

Work even on these stitches for 2½ (3)" [6 (7.5 cm)].
Bind off.

CUFF

To assemble, sew both sides of the heel flap to the foot of the slipper. Fold toe flap back and sew both sides to foot.
Starting at back seam between heel and left side of foot, with double-pointed needles, pick up 15 (17) stitches along left side, 5 (6) stitches along front, 15 (17) stitches along right side, and 5 (6) stitches along back of slipper—40 (46) stitches in total.
Join in the round, and work 2 rounds in knit 1, purl 1 rib.

Round 3 Work 14 stitches in ribbing, knit 2 stitches together, work 4 stitches in ribbing, knit 2 stitches together, work in ribbing to end.

Round 4 Work 13 stitches in ribbing, purl 2 stitches together, work 4 stitches in ribbing, knit 2 stitches together, work in ribbing to end.

Bind off relatively tightly in ribbing, and weave in ends.

TIE

Using B and crochet hook, crochet a chain 35 (40)" [90 (100) cm] long. Thread through the ribbing, and tie in a bow at the front.

POM-POM SLIPPERS

DESIGNED BY KATE ATHERLEY

KNIT/EASY

A variation of the moccasin slippers (page 102), these flirty pom-pom socks are like cheerleaders for your feet.

SIZE

Women's S (up to shoe size 7);
L (shoe size 7 and up)
Sample shown 9½" long x 10" around ball of foot (24.1 cm x 25.4 cm)

MATERIALS

 LION BRAND® WOOL-EASE® THICK & QUICK®
80% ACRYLIC, 20% WOOL
6 OZ (170 G) 108 YD (98 M) BALL

1 ball each #122 Taupe (A) and #112 Raspberry (B), or colors of your choice

- Set size 11 (8 mm) double-pointed needles, *or size to obtain gauge*
- Large-eyed, blunt needle
- Pom-pom maker

GAUGE

9 stitches and 14 rows = 4" (10 cm) square in stockinette stitch using size 11 (8 mm) double-pointed needles.
Be sure to check your gauge.

CUFF

Using A, cast 18 (20) stitches onto a single needle. Distribute stitches as evenly as possible across 3 needles. Join, being careful not to twist stitches.
Work 2 rounds in knit 1, purl 1 rib, as follows:
*Knit 1, purl 1; repeat from * to end of round.

DIVIDE FOR HEEL

Slide the first 9 (10) stitches onto one needle, the remaining 9 (10) onto another. The first 9 (10) stitches will form the heel.

Knit 1 row on 9 (10) heel stitches. (This is the right side.) Turn.
Work 7 more rows in stockinette stitch, slipping the first stitch of every row.

TURN HEEL

Next row is right side facing.
Foundation Row Knit 6 (7) stitches, slip 1, knit 1, pass the slipped stitch over, turn.
Row 1 Slip 1, purl 3 (4), purl 2 stitches together, turn.
Row 2 Slip 1, knit 3 (4), slip 1, knit 1, pass the slipped stitch over, turn.
Repeat rows 1 and 2 until all the stitches are worked. You'll have 5 (6) stitches, and the right side will be facing.

SHAPE THE GUSSET

Knit the 5 (6) heel stitches. Using a new needle, pick up 5 stitches

9 (10) instep stitches on needle 2, and 8 (8) stitches on needle 3.

Round 1 Knit 1 round, knitting through the back loop of all the picked-up stitches.

Round 2 Needle 1: knit to last 3 stitches, knit 2 stitches together, knit 1; needle 2: knit all 9 (10) stitches; needle 3: knit 1, slip slip knit, knit to the end of the round.

Round 3 Knit.

Repeat rounds 2 and 3 until needles 1 and 3 together have a total of 9 (10) stitches each—18 (20) stitches total.

FOOT

Continuing in stockinette stitch, work even until foot measures 7¾ (9)" (20 [23] cm).

TOE

Round 1 Needle 1, knit to last 3 stitches, knit 2 stitches together, knit 1; needle 2, knit 1, slip slip knit, knit to last 3 stitches, knit 2 stitches together, knit 1; needle 3, knit 1, slip slip knit, knit to end of needle.

Round 2 Knit.

Repeat these last 2 rounds—10 (12) stitches remain. Leaving a 12" (30 cm) tail, cut yarn. Finish by pulling yarn through remaining stitches. Turn sock inside out, and weave yarn tail on the wrong side to secure the end.

POM-POM

Using B, make 2 pom-poms, approximately 2" (5 cm) in diameter. Attach to slippers at the center back of each cuff.

along the first selvedge edge, using the loops created by the slipping in the heel turn.

Using another needle, knit across the 9 (10) instep stitches.

Using another needle again, pick up 5 stitches across the other side, using the loops created by the slipping in the heel turn. Using that same needle, knit 3 from the heel stitches.

The start of the round is now at the center of the heel. Slide the last 3 stitches from the heel onto the next needle so that there are 7 (8) stitches on needle 1, the

CROCHET CHRISTMAS STOCKING

DESIGNED BY ANDI SMITH FOR KNITBRIT

CROCHET/EASY

You can make these stockings in any color you like (even the "traditional" ones seen here). Add bells or buttons, embroider your name across the top, and get ready for Santa.

SIZE

Finished measurements 12" long x 13" around ball of foot (30.5 x 33 cm)

MATERIALS

 LION BRAND® LION® BOUCLÉ
79% ACRYLIC, 20% MOHAIR, 1% NYLON

2½ OZ (70 G) 57 YD (52 M) BALL

2 balls #113 Candy Apple (A), or color of your choice

 LION BRAND® TIFFANY
100% NYLON

1¾ OZ (50 G) 137 YD (125 M) BALL

1 ball #100 White (B), or color of your choice

• Size I-9 (5.5 mm) hook
• Stitch markers
• Large-eyed, blunt needle

GAUGE

Gauge is not critical.

STOCKING

With A, chain 40. Join with slip stitch to form ring.
Working in the round, chain 1, *half double crochet in each chain around; do not join.
Continue working in half double crochet around until leg measures about 8" (20 cm).

HEEL

Row 1 Turn, chain 1, single crochet in first and following 18 single crochet. Join with slip stitch in first single crochet—19 single crochet. Repeat row 1 until heel measures 4½" (11.25 cm). Turn.

TURN HEEL

Row 1 Chain 1, single crochet in first single crochet, (single crochet 2 together) twice, chain 9, (single crochet 2 together) twice, single crochet in last single crochet. Join with slip stitch in first single crochet, turn—15 single crochet.
Row 2 Chain 1, single crochet in first single crochet, (single crochet 2 together) twice, chain 5, (single crochet 2 together) twice, single crochet in last single crochet. Join with slip stitch in first single crochet, turn—11 single crochet.
Row 3 Chain 1, single crochet in first single crochet, (single crochet

2 together) twice, chain 1, (single crochet 2 together) twice, single crochet in last single crochet. Join with slip stitch in first single crochet, turn—7 single crochet.

Row 4 Chain 1, single crochet in first single crochet, single crochet 2 together, chain 1, single crochet 2 together, single crochet in last single crochet. Do not turn—5 single crochet.

Evenly pick up the single crochet: 14 single crochet along left heel flap, place marker, 21 single crochet along stocking instep, place marker, 14 single crochet along right heel flap—54 single crochet.

GUSSET

Working single crochet into each loop, single crochet decreasing thus: Single crochet 2 together, single crochet **before** left heel flap marker and single crochet, single crochet 2 together after right heel flap marker until there are 40 single crochet remaining. Remove markers.

FOOT

Work half double crochet into each loop until foot measures 9" (22.5 cm) from back of heel. Arrange foot so that it lays flat with the top of foot shaping; place marker at either side of foot.

Single crochet 2 together on either side of markers on next and following 3rd round until 20 single crochet remain. Join with a slip stitch and turn inside out. Sew seam closed. Using large-eyed, blunt needle, weave in tail ends.

CUFF

With 2 strands of B, single crochet into each loop at top of leg working in the round until 6" (15 cm) of cuff have been crocheted. Fasten off. Using large-eyed, blunt needle, weave in ends and fold down.

HANGER

With A, chain 25, turn, single crochet into each loop. Fasten off. Fold in half and attach to inside of stocking about 1" (2.5 cm) from the top.

KNIT CHRISTMAS STOCKING

DESIGN BY ANDI SMITH FOR KNITBRIT

KNIT/EASY

Knit yourself an oversized stocking—who knows, maybe Santa will bring you more yarn?

SIZE

Finished measurements 12" long x 13" around ball of foot (30.5 x 33 cm)

MATERIALS

 LION BRAND® LION® BOUCLÉ
79% ACRYLIC, 20% MOHAIR, 1% NYLON
2½ OZ (70 G) 57 YD (52 M) BALL

2 balls #113 Candy Apple (A)

 LION BRAND® TIFFANY
100% NYLON
1¾ OZ (50 G) 137 YD (125 M) BALL

1 ball #100 White (B), or color of your choice

• Set of size 6 (4 mm) double-pointed needles
• Large-eyed, blunt needle

GAUGE

Gauge is not critical.

NOTE

To work with 2 strands of Tiffany from one ball, pull the center thread and the outside thread and use them together.

TOP

Using 2 strands of B, cast on 52 stitches and divide evenly onto 4 needles (13 on each)
Purl 6 rows.

LEG

Switch to A.
Rounds 1–6 Knit.
Round 7 On needles 1 and 3, knit 2 stitches together, knit to end. On needles 2 and 4, knit to last 2 stitches, knit 2 stitches together—48 stitches.
Rounds 8–13 Knit.
Repeat rounds 7–13 twice—40 stitches.
Row 28 Knit 2 stitches together, knit

to last 2 stitches, knit 2 stitches together—38 stitches.
Knit 6 rounds.
Round 35 Repeat round 28—36 stitches.
Round 36 Increase in first stitch on needle 1 and last stitch on needle 4—38 stitches.
Knit 2 rounds.
Round 39 Repeat round 36—40 stitches.

HEEL

Row 1 Knit the stitches on needle 1, turn.
Row 2 Purl the stitches on needles 1 and 4, turn—20 stitches.
Working on these two needles only, and working in stockinette stitch, increasing at end of needle 4 and beginning of needle 1 next and following 4th row—24 stitches.
Knit 2 rows.
Decrease at the end of needle 4

edge, knit across instep stitches, pick up 11 stitches along left edge. Decrease on either side of instep stitches on next and following alternate rounds until there are 8 stitches on needles 1 and 4. Knit 6 rounds.

SHAPE FOOT
Round 1 Knit 2 stitches together at beginning of all 4 needles.
Rounds 2–6 Knit.
Round 7 Decrease at beginning of needles 1 and 3 and end of needles 2 and 4.
Rounds 8–11 Knit.
Repeat rounds 7–11 until 10 stitches remain.
Work 5 rows even.
Break off yarn and thread through remaining stitches and fasten off. Sew the tail through the top of the toe for about 3" (8 cm) in a running stitch and pull tightly to form a curve to the toe.
Weave in all loose ends.

and beginning of needle 1 next and following 4th row—20 stitches. Knit 2 rows.

TURN HEEL
Row 1 Knit 11, knit 2 stitches together, knit 1, turn.

Row 2 Slip 1 purlwise, purl 3, purl 2 stitches together, purl 1, turn.
Row 3 Slip 1, knit 4, knit 2 stitches together, knit 1, turn.
Repeat rows 2 and 3 until all the stitches are worked—12 stitches left. Pick up 11 stitches along right

HANGER
With A, cast on 25 stitches, knit 1 row, bind off. Fold in half and attach to the inside of the stocking about 1" (2.5 cm) down from the cuff.

YARN INDEX

AMISH APRÈS-SKI SOCKS,
SEE PAGE 32

AUTUMN ROADSIDE SOCK,
SEE PAGE 55

BIRD'S EYE CHILDREN'S SLIPPERS,
SEE PAGE 62

BLUEBIRD LACE SOCK,
SEE PAGE 46

CHEVRON LACE SOCKS,
SEE PAGE 51

CROCHET CHRISTMAS STOCKING,
SEE PAGE 106

FAIR ISLE HEART SOCKS,
SEE PAGE 77

THE FOREST AND THE TREES SOCKS,
SEE PAGE 90

HIKING SOCKS, SEE PAGE 30

JOAN'S CROCHETED SOCKS,
SEE PAGE 18

JOAN'S KNITTED SOCKS,
SEE PAGE 15

KNIT CHRISTMAS STOCKING,
SEE PAGE 108

LOUNGE LIZARD SOCK,
SEE PAGE 73

LUCKY 7 SOCKS, SEE PAGE 38

MOCCASIN SLIPPERS,
SEE PAGE 102

MOSS ON THE MOUNTAIN SOCKS,
SEE PAGE 84

NORWEGIAN-STYLE FOOTED
SLIPPERS, SEE PAGE 60

OP ART SOCKS, SEE PAGE 67

POM-POM SLIPPERS,
SEE PAGE 104

PUMPKIN SLIP STITCH SOCK,
SEE PAGE 87

REVERSIBLE CABLE SOCK,
SEE PAGE 35

SQUARES & STRIPES SOCKS,
SEE PAGE 65

SHAPED ARCH SOCK, SEE PAGE 42

STRIPED FOOTIES, SEE PAGE 23

SUMMER WAVE SOCKS,
SEE PAGE 81

TABI SOCKS, SEE PAGE 98

TOELESS PEDICURE SOCK,
SEE PAGE 95

TOE-UP STRIPED SLIPPER SOCKS,
SEE PAGE 26

TRAVELING SOCK, SEE PAGE 21

WHITBY LACE SOCK, SEE PAGE 49

INDEX